THE IMPOSTER SYNDROME WORKBOOK

A Comprehensive Guide to Help You:

- Develop a healthy coping response to mistakes and failures.
- Build your confidence in social situations.
- Reach your goals faster by approaching them the right way.

TONY BENNIS

CONTENTS

INTRODUCTION

Imposter syndrome, originally referred to as 'imposter phenomenon', was first identified in 1978 by psychologists Dr. Suzanne Imes and Dr. Pauline Clance. During their clinical trials on a group of high performing women, Imes and Clance noted a pattern of dissatisfaction, anxiety, self-doubt, and fear of failure exhibited by these women, despite overwhelming evidence of their career and academic success. The high achievers all displayed signs of disbelief about their accomplishments, and they all had intense feelings of worry that they would eventually be exposed as a fraud. These feelings resulted in consistent emotional turmoil, and destructive behavior.

Since the imposter phenomenon was first discovered in the 1970's, it has been confirmed that the feelings of being an imposter were not restricted to one gender but affected high achievers in general. By 2021, there was evidence that close to 70% of highly intelligent and successful people were frequently experiencing feelings of intellectual phoniness and were incapable of internalizing their success. This meant that for the vast majority of people, success did not evoke feelings of happiness.

Mountains of Missed Opportunities

If you are reading this workbook, then chances are you or someone that you know is suffering from imposter syndrome. You have probably seen firsthand how feelings of incompetence, self-doubt, fear of judgement and fear of failure can prevent us 'imposters' from reaching our goals and embracing new opportunities. You have also seen how uncontrolled negative self-talk can wreak havoc on our ability to stay motivated, act and inspire. You understand the exhaustion and isolation that we can experience when fighting these feelings alone, day in and day out.

The sad truth is, most of us are not equipped with the knowledge or the tools to help rid ourselves of the destructive thought and behavioral patterns that are characteristic of imposter syndrome. Luckily, for those of us that have managed to become aware that "something is off", we can begin our journey of self-reflection, self-awareness, self-acceptance, self-healing, and eventually, self-mastery. This workbook aims to help you unmask your internal imposter and shift your perspective so that you can regain control of your life and claim your success!

How Does This Workbook Approach the Issue?

This workbook provides you with a comprehensive, step-by-step approach which addresses the critical areas that imposter syndrome impacts in your life. The workbook is laid out in a structured, practical format, with each chapter incrementally building on the previous ones. It utilizes a series of examples, activities, and metaphors that are aimed at deepening your understanding of each subject area, and helping you to effectively implement these approaches in the critical areas of your life.

An Overview of the Subject Areas Covered in this Workbook

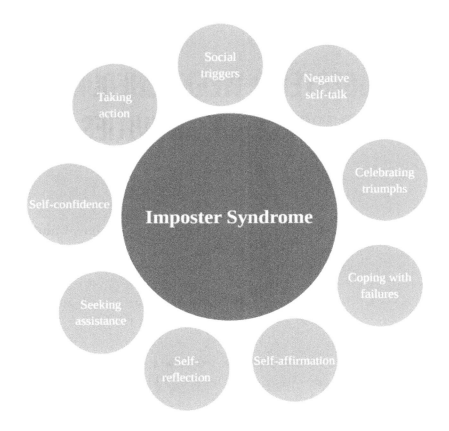

SUGGESTED 8-WEEK SCHEDULE FOR WORKBOOK ACTIVITIES

Week 1. **Read and complete the exercises in chapters 1 and 2.**
- Update your list of specific social situations that trigger your imposter syndrome on a weekly basis, or as needed.
- Practice the mindfulness (visualization) techniques for 10 to 15 minutes each day.

Week 2. **Read and complete the exercise in chapter 3.**
- Practice journaling three small wins for 5 minutes each day.
- Practice celebrating and expressing gratitude for your small wins daily.

Week 3. **Read and complete the exercises in chapter 4.**
- Review the list of social situations that you compiled in week 1 and for each entry, write out any unhealthy coping mechanism responses that you exhibited during those situations.
- List any alternative, healthier coping mechanisms that could have been used in those situations.

Week 4. **Read and complete the exercises in chapter 5.**
- Create or customize at least 3 positive affirmations for each major area of your life (experiences, career, family, finances, body image, education).

- Practice reciting your positive affirmations at least 10-12 times daily (also make it a habit to say a positive affirmation every time you experience a small win).

Week 5.   Read and complete the exercises in chapter 6.
- Practice journaling about a personal event of interest for 15 minutes each day.
- Use the Gibbs six-step model to practice self-reflecting with each journal entry.
- Take 10 minutes to review the list of social situations that you compiled in week 1. Use the Gibbs six-step model to self-reflect on each trigger event.

Week 6.   Read and complete the exercises in chapters 7 and 8.
- Refer to the list of unhealthy coping mechanisms that you compiled for Exercise 4.1. Note the entries that could benefit from seeking guidance and support from friends and family.
- Practice describing yourself objectively in different social settings. Some key areas to look at include your interaction with other people, how you see yourself, and how you think that others see you.

Week 7.   Read and complete the exercises in chapters 9 and 10.
- Practice using implementation intention when setting goals for this week.
- Use commitment devices and micro-actions for goals that require more discipline and/or effort.
- Celebrate your small wins whenever you complete a micro-action.
- Write a self-reflection journal entry about the circumstances that caused you to not complete a micro-action.
- Review the 6 simple steps to become more resilient to life's tough lessons in Chapter 4.

Week 8.   **Finding Patterns and making connections.**
- Review your self-reflection and small wins journal. Note any trends in circumstances, people, feelings, thoughts, and behaviors over the last few weeks.
- Create a schedule to record how many times you are journaling, expressing gratitude, reciting positive affirmations, and completing planned actions weekly.

Chapter 1

INTRODUCTION TO IMPOSTER SYNDROME

Imposter syndrome is the persistent feeling of phoniness and unworthiness that some of us experience when it comes to our own achievements. Imposter syndrome causes us to be convinced that our ideas and skills aren't worthy of other's attention. We constantly seek out ways to discredit ourselves when it comes to our successes. We do this by either focusing on personal flaws to exaggerate or by simply brainwashing ourselves to believe that another person's attributes are somehow more refined than our own. In fact, even our greatest accomplishments are overshadowed by our tiniest mistakes, and this is one of the most prominent characteristics of imposter syndrome.

THE 5 MAIN IMPOSTER SYNDROME PERSONALITIES

Dr. Valerie Young categorized the sufferers of imposter syndrome into five groups: the perfectionists, the superheroes, the natural geniuses, the experts, and the rugged individualists/soloists.

The Perfectionist – Here the individual exhibits perfectionist traits, such as having extremely high and/or unrealistic goals and personal standards. This type of imposter can be excessively critical when self-evaluating and can have a hard time dealing with their own mistakes (as well as the mistakes of others).

The Superheroes – Here the individual is driven to work harder than everyone else in an attempt to feel useful or worthy of their contribution. This individual derives confidence from outperforming others, and as such, they are highly competitive. 'Superheroes' are predisposed to burnout due to overworking.

The Natural Geniuses - Here the individual has a history of high performance in certain areas with very little effort. As a result, they believe that succeeding should be effortless. This type of imposter can feel an immense amount of pressure to prove to the world that they can achieve their goals effortlessly. If 'natural geniuses' cannot do this, they feel like an imposter, which predisposes them to be reluctant to try anything new.

The Experts – Here the individual prides themself on accumulating the most knowledge on a subject area and feels threatened when placed in a situation that questions their expertise. This type of imposter is constantly fearful of being exposed as not being a credible source of information, which drives them to try to learn everything there is to know about their area of expertise.

The Rugged Individualists/Soloist – Here the individual is highly independent and will consider their contribution as invalid if they receive help from others. They will stop at nothing to complete a task themselves, even if the task is impossible to complete alone.

THE STORY OF ERICA AND DANIEL

Let's explore the stories of Erica and Daniel to gain some insight on how imposter syndrome can impact our lives in not-so-obvious ways.

Erica is a thirty-six-year-old office assistant who considers herself to be an introvert. Due to her solitary lifestyle, limited hobbies, and aversion to social activities, she believes that people will regret trying to get to know her, since she lives an "ordinary and uninteresting life". At work, she is always nervous around her colleagues, and she tends to keep to herself out of fear that they may discover that she is actually much less intelligent and competent than them.

Erica's manager offers her a promotion to the new role of office manager. At first, she politely declines because she is afraid that her colleagues will assume that she got the job because of luck or favoritism, and she fears that they will not support her in the new role. Her manager explains that she has been offered the role because she has worked at the company for 5 years, is highly efficient at her job, and had recently acquired a designation which the company considers to be an asset. Erica feels like her manager is exaggerating. But she reluctantly accepts the offer.

The truth is, she doesn't even believe that she is a good office assistant, since she forgot to change the date in the headline of the last report. She is relieved that nobody has discovered her mistake, but she can't shake the looming feeling that they will find out eventually. Lately, she finds herself constantly regretting not having studied earlier on in life, believing that to be the reason she hasn't been as successful as her highly talented colleagues.

Daniel is a forty-one-year-old entrepreneur in the software and technology space. His venture had started with the creation of his YouTube channel called 'Software 101 for Non-Techs', which he has been using to upload videos that describe the application of various trending software for freelance work and academia. His inspiration for the channel comes from a few well-established influencers in the same industry, who have more than one million subscribers and followers on various social media platforms, including YouTube. However, after three years of uploading weekly videos, Daniel has only managed to amass 6,023 subscribers on his YouTube channel.

Daniel decides to start doing live videos explaining complex topics in order to give viewers a chance to ask him questions and receive the answers they need for their unique problems. His first three sessions averaged around 650 to 800 participants at a time. At the start of his fourth live session, he notices that there are 7,700 people waiting to view the session, and he begins to experience feelings of anxiety. Daniel knows that one of the more popular influencers in the software and technology niche averages around 3,200 viewers during their live streams, so he couldn't fathom why he would have a higher turnout than his 'more talented and experienced' competitor. Daniel believes that there must either be some kind of glitch in the numbers, or, if the numbers are correct, that these people must have been misinformed about what to expect.

Daniel nervously presents his insight and expertise on a new topic, and by the end of the live stream he receives immense positive feedback from the session's attendees. Despite this, he can't shake the feeling that these people weren't actually that impressed by his modest content. He starts to wonder if one of his friends had played a cruel prank on him. He doesn't tell anyone about the session's success in order to save himself from potential embarrassment if he finds out that it was all a ruse. During his next session, there is an ever-higher turnout of attendees and Daniel is forced to confide in a friend that he doesn't understand why all of these people would bother to listen to him when there are more qualified people out there speaking about the same subject matter.

Daniel's friend tells him that his presenting technique, charisma, and relatability are so unique, that it is probably the driving force behind his new following. Daniel laughs and brushes it off. He believes that his friend is just being nice to help him calm down.

THE TRUTH ABOUT IMPOSTER SYNDROME

First, let's review Erica's story. Due to her limiting belief that she is an ordinary and/or unremarkable person, she lacks confidence and does not accept that she should be rewarded by management. She ignores her achievement, and instead focuses on a minor error that in her eyes, is a huge problem. Erica is a prime example of someone with a perfectionist personality trait. She does not allow room for mistakes, which is actually an impossible standard to set for oneself. Having unattainable standards is a direct precursor to developing low self-esteem since we feel let down when we do not measure up to our own expectations.

In Daniel's story, he introduces self-imposed limitations on himself because in his eyes his competitors are more qualified than him, and thus should automatically demand the attention and praise of a larger number of viewers. He totally ignores the possibility that he may possess traits that outshine those of his competitors. Even when faced with positive feedback from his viewers (which serves as irrefutable evidence that his skills and knowledge are valued and respected) his mind still finds ways to introduce disbelief. Daniel discredits himself without a second thought, despite the fact that there is little evidence to support his negative thinking.

Negative self-talk is directly associated with feelings of self-doubt, lack of confidence, and fear of failure. Negative self-talk is created by years of negative emotional conditioning, which causes us to have certain negative core beliefs about ourselves that may not always necessarily be true. More often than not, it causes us to develop low self-esteem.

The truth is, if we desperately want to believe something negative, and we think that way often enough, it actually does become our reality. This is why it is so important to expand our self-awareness to become an active participant in observing and vetting our thoughts. In order to deal with imposter syndrome, we must bring our attention to the thinking patterns, events, people, and social situations that trigger feelings of being an imposter within our lives. Let's begin the process by completing **Exercise 1.1.** below.

EXERCISE 1.1 – IDENTIFY THE SITUATIONS THAT TRIGGER YOUR IMPOSTER SYNDROME

Let's start by identifying who we are interacting with and what we are doing when imposter syndrome kicks in. Then, we will focus on identifying the specific events, tendencies and social situations that trigger feelings of unworthiness or inauthenticity within us.

1. Who are you usually talking to when imposter syndrome kicks in? Place an 'X' on the lines associated with the interactions that apply to you.

Strangers _____

Family members _____

Close friends _____

Acquaintances _____

Work Colleagues _____

Boss/supervisor _____

Spouse/significant other _____

Neighbors _____

Trainers/college professors _____

Other: _____ _____

*Review the interaction(s) you have selected, does it pertain to **one person** or **a group of people**? Circle the one that applies.*

2. What are you typically doing when you begin to feel like an imposter? Place an 'X' on the lines associated with the interactions that apply to you.

Asking for help   _____

Making small talk   _____

Sharing personal information   _____

Maintaining a conversation   _____

Trying to make a suggestion to someone   _____

Trying to explain technical information   _____

Trying to express your emotions/feelings   _____

Talking to someone in person/ face to face   _____

Talking to someone remotely (Eg. over the telephone)   _____

Expressing disagreement about something   _____

Other: _____   _____

3. Here is a list of some social situations that may trigger feelings of self-doubt and lack of confidence. Place an 'X' on the lines associated with the social situations that apply to you.

Public speaking _____

Taking an exam _____

Receiving compliments _____

Working out at a public gym _____

Talking about your achievements _____

Other: _____ _____

Performing tasks in front of others _____

Giving your opinion/advice to others _____

Introducing yourself in a group setting _____

Asking a question in a group setting _____

Being questioned (Eg. In a job interview) _____

4. Here is a list of some tendencies that can be associated with our own limited belief systems and are often signs that we may be placing self-imposed limitations on ourselves. Place an 'X' on the lines associated with the tendencies that apply to you.

You are always waiting for the right time to do something.   _____

You are generally unwilling to take risks.   _____

You prefer to stay in your comfort zone.   _____

You tend to focus on your shortcomings.   _____

You are not consistent when it comes to your goals.   _____

You tend to give up on things before starting them.   _____

You tend to make assumptions about what others are thinking.   _____

You are not open to receiving new information.   _____

You tend to underestimate yourself.   _____

You tend to overestimate others.   _____

Other tendencies: _____   _____

5. Here is a list of some events that may act as the catalyst which causes you to experience a fear of failure. Place an 'X' on the lines associated with the tendencies that apply to you.

Awaiting feedback about a test   _____

Receiving additional responsibilities at work   _____

Competitive activities (Eg. Playing sports)   _____

Enrolling in a degree program   _____

Learning to drive   _____

Becoming a parent   _____

Starting a new job   _____

Starting a business   _____

Getting married   _____

Learning a new skill   _____

Other event: _____   _____

SAMPLE EXERCISE 1.2 – LIST THE TOP THREE SOCIAL SITUATIONS THAT LEAD TO FEELINGS OF BEING AN IMPOSTER

Erica:

1. *Asking for help from work colleagues.*
2. *Sharing personal information with strangers.*
3. *Giving her opinion/advice to acquaintances.*

Daniel:

1. *Trying to explain something important to a large group of people.*
2. *Receiving compliments from others about his accomplishments.*
3. *Talking about his achievements with close friends.*

Use Erica's and Daniel's examples as a guide to help you identify your own top three social situations that make you feel like an imposter. Feel free to combine all of the choices you have made thus far as you try to narrow down the situations that affect you the most.

EXERCISE 1.2 – LIST THE TOP THREE SOCIAL SITUATIONS THAT LEAD TO FEELINGS OF BEING AN IMPOSTER

Describe three social situations that are the most problematic when it comes to feelings of imposter syndrome in your life:

1. _____

2. _____

3. _____

Chapter 2

UNDERSTANDING
YOUR FEELINGS

For those of us who are suffering from imposter syndrome, it is extremely challenging to accept that our feelings of inadequacy might simply be the result of our persistent, unchecked negative thoughts. This is because we have evolved to find ways to convince ourselves that we aren't engaging in negative self-talk at all! Our emotional mind employs yet another creative tactic to exercise control over our behavior by camouflaging negative self-talk as something else – constructive criticism!

The problem is, many of us didn't get the memo that constructive criticism isn't meant to demotivate us, depress us, highlight our flaws, or mock us in our failings. In fact, what we have just described are actually different forms of destructive criticism. So how is it that our brain manages to disguise such negativity as being helpful and logical? The answer to this question is very simple, yet extremely difficult to correct.

THE EMOTIONAL MIND VS THE RATIONAL MIND

The problem is that more often than not, we tend to zone out and operate as if running on 'autopilot' while navigating through our daily activities. If you take a back seat when it comes to matters of the mind, whenever a situation arises, the emotional mind will dominate the rational mind each and every time.

The emotional mind is ruled by feelings and emotions. It is directly linked to our basic survival instincts and is the form of thinking that kicks in automatically. The rational mind is ruled by logic and probabilities. It requires more focus and mental effort on our part for it to kick into action.

Let's explore the types of thoughts that arise from the rational mind vs the emotional mind.

Emotional Thinking	**Rational Thinking**
He is the same age as me, but he is successful, and I am not. I will probably never be successful at this rate, I am so useless.	His success has nothing to do with my own self-worth. Success is not a finite resource, and there is room for me to achieve success in my own endeavors.
I feel guilty that I turned down my friend's dinner invitation. She probably thinks that I am inconsiderate and is upset with me.	I declined the invitation because I am feeling emotionally drained and would like to recharge by spending some time alone. I am not being selfish for making a decision that prioritizes my mental health.

I feel afraid that my classmates will look down on me if they find out that my parents work minimum wage jobs.

I do not have control over my family's financial situation. Neither do I have control over anyone's reaction to my family's social status. I should focus my attention towards things that I can control.

I am furious that my friend would lie to me about something so important. I am not interested in hearing their explanation, nor do I want an apology.

I should probably listen to their side of the story in case they have a valid reason for making a suboptimal decision. People often make poor decisions when they have limited information.

For the person who isn't very self-aware, emotional thinking will always set the tone for their thoughts, decisions, and actions. However, emotional thinking can often bury us in a mountain of negative thoughts that are often exaggerated and based on pure assumption. In order for us to stop the downward spiral of negative, emotionally driven thoughts, our rational mind has to actively decode these emotional thoughts and introduce reason and evidence-based judgement.

But how much of a role do emotions play when it comes to our thinking patterns and decision-making processes? Let's review how the body instinctively reacts to the six basic types of human emotions.

AN OVERVIEW OF HOW OUR BODY PHYSICALLY RESPONDS TO THE SIX BASIC TYPES OF EMOTIONS

American psychologist Paul Ekman proposed that as human beings, we experience six primary types of emotions, namely: happiness, anger, sadness, fear, surprise, and disgust. Each of these emotions are directly linked to the body's three main neurotransmitters as follows:

Neurotransmitter	Linked Emotion
Adrenaline	Anger, fear, surprise
Dopamine	Happiness
Serotonin	Sadness, disgust

It is the unique combination of these neurotransmitters that produces the wide range of other emotions we may encounter as part of the human experience, such as shame, pride, excitement, sympathy, confusion, satisfaction, and embarrassment.

Our emotions also cause our body to increase or decrease the production of certain hormones. For example, cortisol is one of the hormones which increases when we become angry or afraid. Increases in adrenaline and cortisol cause our heart rate, blood pressure, perspiration levels and body temperature increase, our muscles tense up, and our breathing becomes erratic. When we are sad, estrogen and progesterone levels lower alongside serotonin levels, which causes us to experience stomach upset, have a lack of appetite, suffer from insomnia, tiredness, back and join pain, and experience weight loss and/or weight gain.

EXERCISE 2.1 - YOU ARE NOT YOUR THOUGHTS: TAKING BACK CONTROL BY INCREASING SELF-AWARENESS

This exercise aims to help you increase your self-awareness when it comes to your negative thoughts and thinking patterns. In this exercise, you observe your thoughts in an objective way, and you learn to intentionally disconnect from the automatic emotional responses that can arise when you are not actively being self-aware.

Let's start by using a visualization technique that can help us to recognize that we are separate from our thoughts:

Visualization Exercise #1: *Imagine that you are standing under a massive waterfall. The water is pouring down on your head, drenching your hair and clothes. It does this relentlessly, without stopping. At some point, the force of the water begins to push you around, and even tries to drag you down with the current. Imagine staying under the waterfall for so long that you begin to feel like you are part of it, at the whim and mercy of its relentless force.*

Now imagine walking out from under the waterfall and standing near to it. You observe the waterfall and marvel at its intensity and persistence. You quietly acknowledge that you and the waterfall are separate. You know without a doubt that you are not the water.

Your thoughts and constant mind chatter are the waterfall. Negative, positive, and neutral thoughts are all cascading down in your mind at all times. However, practicing mindfulness will help you to regain control and not be dragged down when the current becomes overpoweringly strong with negative self-talk.

Let's continue with another visualization technique aimed at helping you to separate from negative and impulsive thoughts during situations that promote imposter syndrome.

Visualization Exercise #2: *Find a quiet environment with as little distractions as possible. Get yourself into a comfortable position but ensure that you are sitting upright using good posture. Relax your shoulders and bring your attention to your breath. Imagine any tension you have slowly leaving your body with every exhale. Let your breathing happen naturally, don't worry about trying to control the rhythm.*

Slowly begin to recall a specific circumstance or social situation that is of interest to you. Focus on reimagining the event with clarity. Carefully create a clear image of who you are with, where you are and what you are doing.

Use your awareness to perceive the thoughts and other mind chatter that were arising in your mind at the time of the event. Simply observe these thoughts in the same way that you would observe a show on television. Don't try to analyze the content of these thoughts, and do not give energy to any emotions that may be involuntarily triggered by the act of recalling these events. Simply observe these thoughts as if they are clouds floating through clear skies and let them pass by as easily as they arrived.

Practice these visualization techniques for just 15 minutes every day to help to relieve excessive mind chatter and manage the anxiety and stress that can accompany imposter syndrome.

SAMPLE EXERCISE 2.2 – LIST THE POSITIVE THOUGHT TO YOUR NEGATIVE THOUGHTS

Negative Thought	Positive Thought
Erica: I don't really deserve this promotion, I received it out of sheer luck.	Erica: I deserve this promotion because I am highly educated and experienced.
Erica: My relationship will probably fail soon because my partner will find someone who is more attractive and successful.	Erica: My relationship will be a long and happy one because I am a genuine person, who is very caring and has a lot of other positive attributes to bring to the table.
Daniel: I can't believe I was selected for first prize as the best visual artist of the year, I probably benefitted from someone's error.	Daniel: I was selected as visual artist of the year due to my unique ideas and approaches. It has also been the result of countless hours of practice, and trial and error.
Daniel: I will never be able to lose weight no matter how hard I try, I should just give up.	Daniel: If I put in consistent effort, I will achieve the weight-loss results that I desire, even if it is a slow process.

EXERCISE 2.2 – LIST THE POSITIVE THOUGHT TO YOUR NEGATIVE THOUGHTS

Negative Thought	**Positive Thought**

1 _____   _____
  _____   _____
  _____   _____
  _____   _____

2 _____   _____
  _____   _____
  _____   _____
  _____   _____

3 _____   _____
  _____   _____
  _____   _____
  _____   _____

4 _____   _____
  _____   _____
  _____   _____
  _____   _____

Chapter 3

CELEBRATING YOUR SMALL WINS

A small win is any triumph, success, or achievement, no matter how small. For some of us, a small win can be sticking to our diet or fitness plan for a few weeks. For others, a small win can be something as simple as making our bed in the morning. There are no set criteria for what a small win should be. What is important is that we give ourselves credit for the effort that we have put in, and all effort counts. Think of it this way, if we are helping an infant learn to walk, we extend the grace and patience needed to help the child take each step, and we encourage them to try again if they fall. We cheer and celebrate every step because we know it will give them the confidence and motivation to keep going. After all, we know that the effort will pay off when they learn to walk and run. Similarly, we need to extend grace and patience to ourselves when it comes to our small wins. This means that we should take the lead and cheer ourselves on for doing a great job, especially for the little things.

In today's society, social media has conditioned us to place more value in the wins of others, as opposed to our own accomplishments. Furthermore, we have gotten used to only celebrating huge, impersonal victories, like our team winning a football match, or our favorite actor/actress winning an Oscar. Yet, when it comes to celebrating our own small victories, we suddenly feel like it's self-centered. Or we diminish the value of these successes as something insignificant. For those of us that suffer from imposter syndrome, we experience this feeling in a notably pronounced way.

It doesn't help the situation that our brain actually has something called a 'negative bias'. This refers to the tendency of our brain to overly focus on negative experiences, because from an evolutionary perspective, learning from bad experiences in how we've managed to survive. The bad news is, nature has made it easier for us to focus on negativity and negative experiences. The good news is, this negative bias can be brought into balance by expanding our self-awareness. Still, becoming aware of our own negative self-talk is only half the battle. The other half of the battle is to actively engage in positive reinforcement. Consistently giving ourselves positive reinforcement for our small wins helps us to rewire our brain to prioritize positive self-talk, and it is one of the best kept secrets when it comes to beating imposter syndrome.

SAMPLE EXERCISE 3 – CREATING A DAILY JOURNAL TO IDENTIFY AND CELEBRATE OUR SMALL WINS

Writing down your top three achievements every day is a good way to identify your small wins and also get to learn more about yourself. For example, reviewing what you have written at the end of the week/month can reveal critical thought patterns, help you to shift/adjust your priorities and also highlight the things that you should be thankful for (and normally may have taken for granted).

When writing your three daily wins, be sure to include things like:

- Something that you set out to do (eg. I jogged one mile today).
- Something that you are grateful for (eg. My wife cooked a delicious dinner).
- Something that you have accomplished (eg. I completed my online course).

Let's navigate how to use small wins to build confidence, motivation and gratitude, the powerful trifecta that will put even the most stubborn imposter syndrome into remission for good!

Top Three Daily Achievements (Erica)

- I cleaned my bedroom.
- I received a 30% discount on dress for sale.
- I have received my driver's license.

Top Three Daily Achievements (Daniel)

- I went for a walk and enjoyed the fresh air.
- I was able to sleep through the night (no insomnia).
- I successful completed a business presentation to IT professionals.

EXERCISE 3 – CREATING A DAILY JOURNAL TO IDENTIFY AND CELEBRATE OUR SMALL WINS

Before you get started, let's review a shortlist of 30 examples of common small wins that are worthy of attention, praise, and gratitude.

Small Wins to Keep on Your Radar

1. Woke up early.
2. Learned a new skill.
3. Ate a healthy meal.
4. Tried something new.
5. Felt inspired.
6. Drank enough water to stay hydrated.
7. Trusted your intuition.
8. Motivated a friend.
9. Tidied up your room.
10. Arrived at a meeting on time.
11. Finished a task ahead of schedule.
12. Had a good idea.
13. Took a break to unwind.
14. Performed an act of self-care.
15. Performed an act of compassion.
16. Exercised for 30 minutes.
17. Saved $20.
18. Finished a novel.
19. Had the courage to ask for help.
20. Spent quality time with spouse/children/parents/siblings.
21. Rested.
22. Did the laundry.
23. Did not procrastinate.
24. Took a shower.
25. Worked on a DIY project.
26. Mowed the lawn.
27. Studied for 1 hour.
28. Meditated.
29. Watered the plants.
30. Found the silver lining in a challenging situation.

Now it's time for you to list your own small wins for each day of the week:

Day of the Week	Three Small Accomplishments
Sunday	_____ _____
Monday	_____ _____
Tuesday	_____ _____
Wednesday	_____ _____
Thursday	_____ _____
Friday	_____ _____
Saturday	_____ _____

Remember that over time, even the smallest daily progressions add up to become huge successes. So, whenever you experience a small triumph, freeze. Take time to bask in your accomplishment, no matter how small. Our brain tends to trick us into believing that the next thing on our to-do list will bring greater satisfaction than what we are achieving right now. However, that is hardly ever the case. Our attention should always be focused on the present, not on the past (which is usually a sign of regret), or the future (which is usually a sign of anxiousness).

Furthermore, celebrating your small wins doesn't have to be a grand production either. It can be something as simple as telling a close friend or family member about your achievement. Or you can even celebrate by letting your mind wander to reimagine your achievements, or dream about reaching new successes. Finally, remember to express gratitude for each and every achievement.

Chapter 4

MANAGING CHALLENGES AND SETBACKS

Our ability to cope with the obstacles, delays, and burdens that life throws our way can largely determine the kind of outlook that we adopt in everyday life. However, the reality is that not everyone has the inner strength and resilience to bounce back when faced with major challenges and misfortunes. Even small misfortunes can cause some of us to crumble if they are persistent enough.

In fact, if you tend to feel like an imposter when it comes to acknowledging your own accomplishments, then you are probably very familiar with the nagging feeling that you will never be good enough to be successful or reach your goals. Fear of failure is one of the most crippling characteristics of imposter syndrome because when we fail, which most of us often do, we tend to focus intensely on the negative aspects of the experience. Rather than learn from our failures and keep at it, we become buried in negative self-talk, we dwell on the mistake, and many of us might even develop unhealthy coping mechanisms.

A coping mechanism refers to the actions that we take when we deal with problems, stress, pressure and/or uncomfortable emotions. These actions can be deliberate, or unconscious, as well as healthy or unhealthy. Healthy coping mechanisms tend not to provide instant gratification but can give a long-term positive effect. For example, using exercise as a coping mechanism to relieve daily stress. Unhealthy coping mechanisms tend to give us instant gratification but can have long-term negative effects. For example, smoking as a coping mechanism to relieve daily stress.

EXAMPLE #1 - SCENARIO THAT DEMONSTRATES AN UNHEALTHY COPING MECHANISM

Erica is upset that her manager overlooked her for a promotion to the role of Human Resources Officer. She is not confident enough to discuss the issue with her manager, so she is unable to identify the specific reasons for management's decision. She imagines various scenarios in which her boss might have been hinting at her incompetence, and she becomes even more upset by this.

She buys some chocolate ice-cream from the grocery store and indulges as she seeks comfort during her time of emotional distress. She continues to construct scenarios in her mind and before she knows it, she has eaten three medium-sized containers of ice-cream. Although she enjoyed the experience of eating her favorite food, her disappointments about work remain unresolved.

EXAMPLE #2 - SCENARIO THAT DEMONSTRATES AN UNHEALTHY COPING MECHANISM

Daniel does not like when his spouse goes out with her friends. One day, she tells him that she will be going out to lunch with her friends, followed by spending the day out shopping. He covertly tries to control her by insulting her outfit and criticizing her friends. He arbitrarily lists a set of household tasks that he believes are more important than leisure activities, and he demands that she stay at home.

His wife hesitantly submits to his demands and cancels the outing with her friends. Daniel feels a sense of relief. He always imagines scenarios in which his wife is courted by a more successful suitor during a chance encounter while she is out with her friends. Daniel uses his aggression as a coping mechanism to avoid the uncomfortable feeling of jealousy.

Let's explore some common examples of healthy and unhealthy coping mechanisms using Erica and Daniel as examples.

	Healthy Coping Mechanisms		Unhealthy Coping Mechanisms	
	Erica	*Daniel*	*Erica*	*Daniel*
1.	Meditation techniques	Working out	Over-eating	Drinking alcohol
2.	Problem solving	Social support	Self-harm	Being aggressive
3.	Getting a massage	Taking a break	Social withdrawal	Procrastination

EXERCISE 4.1 – LIST THREE HEALTHY AND UNHEALTHY COPING MECHANISMS THAT YOU USE WHEN YOU EXPERIENCE PARTICULAR EVENTS/SOCIAL SITUATIONS THAT CAUSE STRESS, SETBACKS, FAILURES AND/OR DISAPPOINTMENTS

List of Healthy Coping Mechanisms

Event/Social Situation　　　　　　**Event/Social Situation**

1 _____　　_____

　　_____　　_____

　　_____　　_____

　　_____　　_____

2 _____　　_____

　　_____　　_____

　　_____　　_____

　　_____　　_____

3 _____　　_____

　　_____　　_____

　　_____　　_____

　　_____　　_____

List of Unhealthy Coping Mechanisms

Event/Social Situation   **Event/Social Situation**

1 _____   _____

   _____   _____

   _____   _____

   _____   _____

2 _____   _____

   _____   _____

   _____   _____

   _____   _____

3 _____   _____

   _____   _____

   _____   _____

   _____   _____

EXERCISE 4.2 – ASSESS YOUR LEVEL OF VULNERABILITY TO UNHEALTHY COPING MECHANISMS

Determining your level of resilience is a good way to figure out how predisposed you are to unhealthy coping mechanisms. It's also a sensible place to start when trying to manage how you deal with challenges and setbacks.

Answer the following questions as honestly as you can (be sure to select the option that best describes yourself):

1. Do you feel fulfilled in your job/work?

   ( ) Yes   ( ) No   ( ) Not Sure

2. Do you feel fulfilled in your personal life?

   ( ) Yes   ( ) No   ( ) Not Sure

3. Is your outlook of the world generally positive?

   ( ) Yes   ( ) No   ( ) Not Sure

4. Do you have time for activities that you enjoy? For example, cycling outdoors or spending quality time with family?

   ( ) Yes   ( ) No   ( ) Not Sure

5. Do you usually find/create solutions when experiencing tough challenges?

   ( ) Yes   ( ) No   ( ) Not Sure

6. Are you comfortable asking for help from family members, close friends, or coworkers?

   ( ) Yes   ( ) No   ( ) Not Sure

7. Do you routinely practice self-care activities? Such as eating healthy meals, getting sufficient sleep and moderate amounts of exercise?

( ) Yes   ( ) No   ( ) Not Sure

8. Do you feel like you are growing as a person?

( ) Yes   ( ) No   ( ) Not Sure

9. Do you think that you adapt to change easily?

( ) Yes   ( ) No   ( ) Not Sure

10. When you experience stress, do you direct your attention to more beneficial activities?

( ) Yes   ( ) No   ( ) Not Sure

If your response was "Yes" for 8 or more out of the 10 questions mentioned above, then chances are you are a very resilient person. You are not easily predisposed to unhealthy coping mechanisms, even during difficult situations, and generally prefer to utilize healthy ones instead.

If your response was "Yes" for between 6 to 7 questions, then chances are you can be more resilient in some parts of your life than others. You may succumb to unhealthy coping mechanisms under more extreme circumstances, but you will successfully navigate your challenges and disappointments the majority of the time.

If your response was "Yes" to 5 or less out of the 10 questions mentioned above, then chances are you can get overwhelmed by life's challenges and disappointments more easily than others. You might have a harder time recovering from major setbacks in life and you have a higher likelihood of being predisposed to more extreme forms of unhealthy coping mechanisms (for example, drug addictions).

BECOME MORE RESILIENT TO LIFE'S TOUGH LESSONS USING THESE 6 SIMPLE STEPS:

1. Embrace your small wins daily, which will serve as the positive reinforcement and support you need for even bigger wins further down the line. Never dismiss a win as being too small.

   Imagine that each small win represents a single brick. Celebrating each small win lays the brick on your mental 'foundation' and repeating the process each day will eventually build a home in your mind where positive thoughts reside. The effort that you put into laying these bricks will determine whether you build a mansion, or just a quaint little house on the prairie.

2. Try to be open minded enough to learn from your experiences and accept verifiable new information that challenges your typical point of view. If you are dead set on holding on to your limiting beliefs and rigid mindset, then that is a sign that you are not ready to free yourself from the woes of imposter syndrome.

   You have to be willing to accept that some aspects of your current mindset are outdated/obsolete and are no longer serving you. As human beings, change can be a little confusing and disorienting, but it's always best to approach change deliberately, with an open mind.

3. Don't be afraid to seek support from close friends, family, or even a qualified professional. It's amazing how many of us are secretly afraid to communicate with those around us out of fear that we may be pitied, ostracized, misunderstood or become some kind of burden to the listener.

   What's even more amazing is that half of the time, none of these dreaded situations ever occur. These fears are usually our own assumptions and speculations about how we expect the particular outcome of a situation will be. However, do not underestimate the grip that imposter syndrome can have over your thinking, decisions, actions, and your quality of life in general.

Yes, it's possible to beat imposter syndrome alone, but it's also possible to punch a bear in a fist fight. Just because it's possible doesn't mean that we should choose to do it (unless of course, you enjoy fighting bears).

4. Use positive affirmations as a way to rewire your brain to seek out the positive things that can happen in your life. We can't always be waiting on something to happen that we can classify as a small win. Sometimes we need to purposefully place a seed of positivity into our subconscious mind, knowing that eventually it will bear fruit.

5. Prioritize self-care. It's a well-known fact that when you feel good on the outside, you feel good on the inside, and vice versa. An action as simple as taking a shower has the potential to stop your spiral into depression in its tracks.

    If you can't find the energy to shower, try just brushing your teeth. Can't do that either? Just breathe in, breathe out, and give yourself time to rest and replenish the energy needed to take one small action at a time.

    It's a well-known fact that people who eat healthily, exercise, get adequate rest, have a hobby, travel, and socialize always seem to have a reserve of energy that us 'imposters' can't figure out where it came from.

6. Keep busy as much as possible, don't give yourself time to dwell on your failures. This doesn't mean that you shouldn't take breaks or find some time to relax. What it means is that if you find yourself sitting and wallowing in self pity over your

problems, you are not relaxing. It would be better to focus your attention to activities that are within your control and are more beneficial to you.

The most important thing to remember throughout this entire process is that we are not inherently born with the ability to be highly resilient during situations that represent major challenges and setbacks. Those persons who have been fortunate enough to experience enough love and support (both mentally and physically) throughout their childhood and young-adult lives to confidently navigate through life's challenges shouldn't take it for granted that others have to fight to equip themselves with the tools needed to safely make it through life's hardships.

Luckily, if you have the right guidance, it's less of a fight and more like a pleasantly transformational experience. This type of lesson doesn't make your failures or hardships magically disappear, but instead it expands your awareness enough to begin to view them differently.

If you can view your setbacks in a healthy way, then you will be able to respond to each unique situation in a way that yields the best outcome for yourself and those around you.

Chapter 5

THE POWER OF AFFIRMATIONS

An affirmation is a statement that we make to ourselves about something that we believe to be true. These statements can be positive, negative, or neutral. For example, "I will never lose weight" is an example of a negative affirmation. Conversely, "I will lose weight through effort and dedication", is an example of a positive affirmation. A neutral affirmation then, would be worded like "Losing weight is possible with enough effort". Positive self-affirmations are beneficial phrases that we use to reinforce our positive thinking, boost our confidence, and motivate ourselves to achieve the best results from any task that we set our mind to do.

Unfortunately, many persons are skeptical about if positive affirmations actually work, or whether it is just another form of useless pseudoscience. Well, look at it this way, those of us with imposter syndrome are intimately familiar with negative self-talk and the barrage of negative self-affirmations that we consciously make as a result. If you have already completed the exercises in chapters 1 to 4, then you are also aware that you make negative self-affirmations on a subconscious level too. Us 'imposters' have seen firsthand the devastating impact that negative self-affirmations can have on our lives. This is because self-affirmation, whether positive or negative, is a powerful weapon that we often use against ourselves, rather than to protect ourselves.

The neuroscience behind self-affirmation is that the neuroplasticity of our brains can be 'trained' to create and maintain connections, much in the same way that a bodybuilder can create and maintain a muscular physique. In fact, there couldn't be a better example of how affirmations work: it's like training your mind to become 'fit' and 'powerful'. This example highlights the long-term benefits of repetition. You don't simply wake up one morning with the physique of a bodybuilder. You start off as a regular person with a goal. However, it is only after weeks and even months of physical effort and repetition that you will reap the benefits that you so desire. Similarly, practicing self-affirmation over several months can strengthen your brain's chemical pathways, and reinforce its neural connections. Of course, becoming a fit and powerful negative thinker is what we 'imposters' are experts at. However, we stand to benefit greatly if we disrupt the existing pattern of negative thinking and reprogram our brains to work for us, not against us.

According to social psychologist Claude M. Steele, when situations occur that threaten our sense of self, we either rationalize what happened in a defensive way, or affirm our own capabilities in order to view the situation objectively. This concept is known as 'self-affirmation theory', and it describes our capacity to change moral outcomes and remain adaptable during situations that threaten our narratives about ourselves. Self-affirmation theory also highlights the importance of becoming competent at the things that give us the deepest insecurities, since this is how we are able to truly view ourselves as being moral, capable and flexible. If we approach using affirmations in this way, any positive affirmations that we present to ourselves will be authentic, since they allow us to resonate and internalize with what we are telling ourselves is true.

For example, it is not practical to use the affirmation "I am the best doctor in the state", if you are not practicing medicine. Likewise, it is pointless to use the affirmation "I will receive the top grade in this exam", if you did not study, or otherwise prepare for the test. Luckily, people that suffer from imposter syndrome are less likely to engage in this kind of toxic positivity (that is, badly structured positive affirmations). However, us 'imposters' are also going to miss out on the benefits of well-structured positive self-affirmations, since we are less likely to believe the affirmation to be true.

The most effective positive self-affirmations are not the generic ones you find around the internet, but are personalized statements that are based on your own unique circumstances.

HOW TO CONSTRUCT A QUALITY POSITIVE SELF-AFFIRMATION

First, identify an important area in your life that you would like to improve. For positive self-affirmation to be effective, we must genuinely feel like we deserve what we are stating. So, this chosen improvement needs to be consistent with your core values. Erica has chosen the following positive self-affirmation:

"I am knowledgeable and competent."

This is a good example of a properly structured positive affirmation since it includes the following criteria:

It starts with 'I'.

Starting your affirmations with 'My' or 'I' personalizes the statement by directing it towards yourself. For example, saying "I am an innovative thinker", is better than saying "Innovative thoughts are entering my mind".

It is worded in the present tense.

Saying "I will be an expert in my field" has a completely different connotation than saying "I am an expert in my field". The term 'will' suggests that you have not accomplished the task as yet, and reinforces the reality that the opposite statement is true. However, the term 'am' suggests that you are currently accomplishing the task, which wires your brain to confirm that you are already achieving what you have set out to do. This concept is not merely a play on words. If you affirm that you are an expert in your field, and you are currently doing things that support being an expert in your field, then using the term 'am' is authentic and will resonate with you on a subconscious level.

It is feasible and achievable.

You need to make sure that you are using positive self-affirmations that are realistic. A blind person can affirm "I am capable of seeing the faces and features of those around me", but this technically wouldn't be possible unless their situation could be reversed by a medical procedure. It would be much better then to affirm "I am capable of connecting with those around me".

It is simple and easy to remember.

One important aspect of applying affirmations effectively is reciting them often. The best way to do this is by using phrases that are easy to recall at any time, anywhere. For example, "I can count on my family to listen, guide and care for me through any difficult situations that life may throw at me" is a decent positive self-affirmation, but it is not as easy to recall and recite as "I can depend on my family to support me", which is an equally effective statement.

EXAMPLES OF POSITIVE AFFIRMATIONS FOR IMPOSTER SYNDROME

Here are a few general examples of positive self-affirmations that others have used to promote positive self-talk and achieve success in various aspects of their lives:

For the Office

"I have a natural born talent for leadership:
"I am knowledgeable, reliable and competent."
"My expertise is valuable and vital to the business."
"I can problem-solve through any challenge that comes my way."
"My performance is worthy of praise and acknowledgement."

For Students

"I am a great learner."
"I can achieve anything that I set out to do."
"My capacity to learn and grow is endless."
"I enjoy studying and learning new things."
"I am proud of my dedication and flexibility."

For Body Positivity

"I am healthy and strong."
"My body deserves love and kindness."
"My beauty is more than skin deep."
"I love and accept my body the way it is."
"My body has helped me achieve amazing things."

For Relationships

"I am worthy of love and affection."

"I support my partner because my partner supports me."

"I am grateful to be loved and cherished by my wife/husband."

"I experience an abundance of love wherever I go."

"I can effortlessly attract the person who is just right for me."

For Low Self-Esteem

"My happiness is not dependent on external circumstances."

"I am grateful for all the good things that happen in my life."

"I am making the best decisions with the limited information that I have."

"I love every aspect of myself."

"My patience and calmness are my superpower."

SAMPLE EXERCISE 5 – CREATING YOUR OWN POSITIVE AFFIRMATIONS

List five areas of your life that you would like to change/improve. Rank each item by order of importance. Here is what Erica has listed:

	Area Selected for Change/Improvement	Rank
1.	My experiences.	3
2.	My relationship with my family.	2
3.	My finances.	4
4.	My body image.	1
5.	My education.	5

Now, choose the top three areas that you would like to focus on. What would you like to change/improve about these areas?

1.	**My body image.**
	I would like to start eating healthier and lose 40 pounds with consistent exercise.
2.	**My relationship with my family.**
	I would like to spend more time with my family and do more activities with them.
3.	**My experiences.**
	I would like to travel the world, starting with a trip to Italy.

Let's look at each area in more detail. List three actions that you can do to create the change listed in each area:

1.	**My body image.**
	I would like to start eating healthier and lose 40 pounds with consistent exercise.

	Be disciplined with portion control.
	Cut out carbs and refined foods.
	Jog for 30 minutes every morning.

2.	**My relationship with my family.**
	I would like to spend more time with my family and do more activities with them.

	Invite parents over for dinner on Wednesdays and Fridays.
	Take nephew bike riding on Saturdays.
	Visit granddad on evenings to chat and water his plants.

3.	**My experiences.**
	I would like to travel the world, starting with a trip to Italy.

	Save $300 monthly towards my travelling expenses.
	Take a beginning course in speaking Italian.
	Get visa documentation prepared/updated.

Now that you are aware of what changes/improvements are most important to you, as well as what you need to do to get started, your task is to select a single action at a time and work towards each sub-goal, until you attain your main goal. In the meantime, you can create supporting positive self-affirmations to help manifest your goals. Let's examine how Erica uses the information she has gathered thus far to create some positive self-affirmation statements that she can use to achieve her top three goals.

Goal No. 1 – My Body Image

- I am the best version of myself.
- My actions support a healthy lifestyle.
- I am excited to be achieving my body goals.

Goal No. 2 – My Relationship with My Family

- I can effortlessly connect and communicate with my family.
- My family loves and respects me.
- I can feel safe to freely express myself with my family.

Goal No. 3 – My Experiences

- I deserve to experience all the world has to offer.
- I am open to learning new things.
- My experiences are unique and memorable.

EXERCISE 5 – CREATING YOUR OWN POSITIVE AFFIRMATIONS

List five areas of your life that you would like to change/improve. Rank each item by order of importance.

	Area Selected for Change/Improvement	**Rank**
1.		
2.		
3.		
4.		
5.		

Choose the top three areas that you would like to focus on. What would you like to change/improve about these areas?

1.	
2.	
3.	

Look at each area in more detail. List three actions that you can do to create the change listed for each area:

1.	

•	
•	
•	

2.	

•	
•	
•	

3.	

•	
•	
•	

Create supporting positive self-affirmations to help manifest your selected goals. Don't forget to select a single action at a time and work towards each sub-goal until you attain your main goal!

Goal No. 1: _____

- _____
- _____
- _____

Goal No. 2: _____

- _____
- _____
- _____

Goal No. 3: _____

- _____
- _____
- _____

Chapter 6

SELF REFLECTION AND JOURNALING

One of Socrates' most famous quotes is this:

"The unexamined life is not worth living."

According to this famous Greek philosopher, human beings require both personal and spiritual growth in order to find a sense of purpose in the life that they are living. The notion that deep self-contemplation is vital for the human experience is nothing new. In fact, there is an entire discipline dedicated to the act of self-reflection, it's called philosophy. But what is self-reflection and why is it so important as a tool for us 'imposters'?

Self-reflection refers to our ability to look inward and use our own mental faculties of introspection as we try to understand our thoughts, motivations, attitudes, and desires. That is, we review our past actions, present predicament, and future expectations and then we ask ourselves a series of questions aimed to help us to understand why we think, feel, and act the way that we do. Self-reflection, therefore, helps us to scrutinize our life at both a micro and macro level. It requires a tremendous amount of discipline and deliberate thinking, and is the main process used to help us achieve an increase in self-awareness and personal growth.

In short, self-reflection helps us to:

- Increase our emotional intelligence,
- Learn from our experiences,
- Differentiate between knowledge and opinions,
- Distinguish between oneself (one's personal identity) and others,
- Determine how we are impacting the lives of others.

Here are some examples of self-reflective type questions:

- "Why is this outcome so important to me?"
- "Have I been utilizing my spare time to the best of my ability this week?"
- "Am I achieving the goals that I set for myself?"
- "Are these behaviors still serving me after all this time?"
- "Is there a way for me to improve myself as a person?"

Unfortunately, we aren't all imbued with a natural inclination to ask ourselves the right questions at the right time. Thus, achieving the best results from the practice of self-reflection is not as intuitive and straightforward as it might seem.

Professor Graham Gibbs developed a methodical approach to self-reflection by creating a six-step model that shows the process through which it can be achieved. These steps include:

	Name	Meaning	Self-Reflective Question	Example
1.	Description	This question should prompt our recollection of the specific events that we feel need to be evaluated.	What is it that happened exactly?	"I angrily smashed the remote while interacting with my wife tonight."
2.	Feelings	This question identifies the specific emotions that are associated with the particular event.	What feelings and emotions were you experiencing at that time?	"I felt upset, disappointed, and betrayed.
3.	Evaluation	This question isolates the aspect of the event that triggered the particular feelings and emotions.	What was it about the experience that caused these feelings and emotions?	"My wife suggesting that I quit being an entrepreneur to work a 9 to 5 job as an employee."
4.	Analysis	This question determines whether the event constituted a learning experience.	Is there anything that can be learned from the experience?	"Destructive physical actions are not an appropriate solution for expressing myself."
5.	Conclusion	This question determines the best alternate response(s) available for the given situation.	Is there an alternative response that you could have done to give a more desirable outcome?	"I could have just sat down with my wife and made an effort to discuss my fears and concerns with her. In addition, I could have been more upfront with expressing the root causes of my insecurities to her."
6.	Action Plan	This question plans your future responses based on all that you have learned.	If a similar circumstance occurred in the future, how would you respond?	"I will use my words, be honest and exercise restraint during moments of anger."

*Please note: These steps are illustrated by using the example stated in sample exercise 6.1.

One major indicator of a lack of self-reflection is the repeating of past mistakes. Luckily, most of us engage in some form of self-reflection (although some do this more than others) at different stages throughout our lives.

Oftentimes, we contemplate our successes and our failures when we reflect. However, those of us with imposter syndrome tend to have a bias to reflect over our failures. Our trademark is that we do this in a way that is not beneficial to our success, or our own wellbeing.

Journaling is one of the most effective methods to stimulate constructive, unbiased self-reflection, because it allows us to track our experiences over time and notice patterns in our decisions, behaviors, and circumstances.

HOW TO WRITE A SELF-REFLECTION JOURNAL

In general, reflection can occur either during or after an event has occurred. According to American philosopher Donald Schön, these two variations of reflection can be described as:

Reflection On-Action – This occurs after the experience has passed and requires us to retrieve and recall the experience in the form of memories.

Reflection In-Action – This requires us to actively reflect, decide and act while we are currently experiencing the event in question.

Writing a self-reflection journal allows us to identify which life experiences we should prioritize as learning experiences. This helps us to align our future decisions and actions with the lessons and values gained from these experiences. Thus, it improves both our reflection on-action capabilities, as well as our reflection in-action capabilities.

To effectively self-reflect using this method, three simple steps can be used:

Step 1 – Recall the event and carefully write it down in a descriptive way.

Step 2 – Contemplate the event by asking yourself a series of reflective questions.

Step 3 – Conclude by taking any lessons learned from Step 2 and applying them to future events (wherever applicable).

SAMPLE EXERCISE 6.1 – HOW TO WRITE A SELF-REFLECTION JOURNAL ENTRY

Step 1 Instructions: Carefully recall the event and write it down in a descriptive way.

Daniel's Journal Entry: *Today is the final day that I will receive sponsorship from a major supporter, so I visited my local bank to secure funding for the continued operations of my business. During the interview process, the loans officer questioned me about my business's income and expenses. I exaggerated my business income, understated the expenses, and also omitted a portion of the debt payable by the company. In the evening, I told my wife what happened, and she looked concerned but did not ask me too much about it. However, while watching TV later that night, she showed me an advertisement for an office job in IT and suggested that I apply "just in case". I became enraged that she would display such a lack of faith in me and my business. I slammed the remote into the floor out of anger, and she did not speak to me for the rest of the night.*

Step 2 Instructions: Contemplate the event by asking yourself a series of questions.

1. "Why did I lie to the bank about my financials?"

Daniel's Answer: *I am afraid that the bank will decline my loan application, which means that my business might be compromised due to the lack of funding for the operating activities. I am also afraid that my wife will see my looming financial distress as a sign of weakness, which could compromise our marriage.*

2. "Why did I express my anger in a physical way?"

Daniel's Answer: *Sometimes when I experience intense emotions, I don't quite know how to put my feelings into words. So, I instinctively use physical actions as a mechanism to display how I am feeling.*

3. "Why did I feel like my wife's suggestion is a betrayal?"

Daniel's Answer: *I have an underlying fear that she believes I am incapable of being the main character in my own story. As my wife, she should know that I do not want to be just another glorified employee in an office job, but at this rate, things might just end up that way and it terrifies me.*

4. "Was the experience a positive or negative one?"

Daniel's Answer: *It was a very negative experience.*

Step 3: Conclude by taking any lessons learned from step 2 and applying them to future events.

5. "What could I have done differently during the experience/ What could I do differently next time?"

Daniel's Answer: I could have talked to my wife about my insecurities and clarified my negative thoughts with her rather than just making assumptions. Next time, I will use my words, and I will exercise patience and restraint if the topic is a difficult one.

EXERCISE 6.1 – HOW TO WRITE A SELF-REFLECTION JOURNAL ENTRY

Step 1: Carefully recall the event and write it down in a descriptive way.

_____

_____

_____

_____

_____

_____

_____

_____

_____

_____

_____

_____

_____

_____

_____

_____

_____

_____

_____

_____

_____

_____

Step 2: Contemplate the event by asking yourself a series of questions.

1. _____

Your Answer:

_____

_____

_____

_____

_____

_____

_____

_____

_____

_____

_____

_____

_____

_____

_____

_____

_____

_____

_____

_____

_____

2. _____

Your Answer:

3. _____

Your Answer:

_____
_____
_____
_____
_____
_____
_____
_____
_____
_____
_____
_____
_____
_____
_____
_____
_____
_____
_____
_____
_____
_____

4. _____

Your Answer:

Step 3: Conclude by taking any lessons learned from step 2 and applying them to future events.

5. _____

Your Answer:

_____

_____

_____

_____

_____

_____

_____

_____

_____

_____

_____

_____

_____

_____

_____

_____

_____

_____

_____

_____

_____

EXERCISE 6.2 – REFLECTING ON SOME CORE ASPECTS OF THE SELF (HAPPINESS, GOALS AND PERSONAL GROWTH)

Are You Happy?

Let's identify what brings you joy in your life:

1. Our values are the things that we hold dear as being crucial to the way we live, love, and work. What are your values, and do you actively practice them?

_____

_____

_____

_____

_____

_____

_____

2. Can you identify whether there is anything you are currently taking for granted? Be honest.

_____

_____

_____

_____

_____

_____

_____

3. List a few things that you are grateful for in your life:

_____

_____

_____

_____

_____

_____

_____

4. Do you love yourself? Why or why not?

_____

_____

_____

_____

_____

_____

_____

5. What can you do to improve your self-care and self-love?

_____

_____

_____

_____

_____

_____

_____

6. Is your life going in the direction that you dreamed it would?

_____

_____

_____

_____

_____

_____

7. Do you practice prioritizing your well-being first and foremost?

_____

_____

_____

_____

_____

_____

8. What situations or activities give you a burst of energy? What drains you?

_____

_____

_____

_____

_____

_____

Are You Meeting Your Goals?

Let's identify whether you are feeling a sense of purpose in your life:

1. Do you make the necessary time to pursue your goals? How are you using your time?

_____

_____

_____

_____

_____

_____

_____

_____

2. What goals have you accomplished within the last 12 months? Explain why you have, or have not, achieved any goals recently.

_____

_____

_____

_____

_____

_____

_____

_____

3. Are there any habits that might be preventing you from achieving your goals? Be honest.

_____

_____

_____

_____

_____

_____

4. Are there any actions that you could take to help you reach your goals?

_____

_____

_____

_____

_____

_____

5. Why are your goals important to you?

_____

_____

_____

_____

_____

_____

6. Is there anything that you can do to motivate yourself into achieving your goals?

_____

_____

_____

_____

_____

_____

7. Are you a competitive person?

_____

_____

_____

_____

_____

8. Do you celebrate your goals when you achieve them?

_____

_____

_____

_____

_____

_____

Are You Growing as a Person?

Let's identify whether you are growing emotionally and spiritually.

9. List any limiting beliefs that you currently have (if you can think of any).

_____

_____

_____

_____

_____

10. Are you aware of the things you can do to increase your self-awareness?

_____

_____

_____

_____

_____

_____

11. Who are you? Describe yourself.

_____

_____

_____

_____

_____

_____

12. Are you holding on to things in your life that no longer serve you?

_____

_____

_____

_____

_____

_____

13. How often do you step out of your comfort zone?

_____

_____

_____

_____

_____

_____

14. Do you hold yourself accountable for your life?

_____

_____

_____

_____

_____

_____

_____

15. Can you identify one time that you may have been in denial about something?

_____

_____

_____

_____

_____

_____

16. Do you experience regret often? Be honest.

_____

_____

_____

_____

_____

_____

Chapter 7

SEEKING SUPPORT AND ENCOURAGEMENT

W e can all recall at least one time in our lives when we tasked ourselves to help someone out. Whether it was in the form of, for example, recommending our friend for a job, or helping our sibling find a good mechanic, or helping our neighbor lift the groceries out of the driveway, or giving a coworker some advice on how to achieve a better result on their report.

When we hear that our friend got that big job, that our sibling can now drive safely at night, that our neighbor has finally been able to recover from his back problem, or that our coworker wowed the management team with their report presentation – we feel good knowing that we contributed to someone's success. Regardless of the specific task we had to carry out, we do not have expectations of a reward in the form of payment or gifts. Our pleasure is derived from knowing that our actions helped to make someone's life easier in some way.

Now, if the majority of us tried to recall those few times in the past where we needed to ask others for help, we'll realize that our feelings about receiving help from others doesn't quite equate to how we feel about providing it. This is because many of us have greater expectations of ourselves than we do for others. We somehow believe ourselves to be openminded enough to help someone without being judgmental. Yet when the shoe is on the other foot, and we are the ones in need of assistance or support, we suddenly fear that others perceive us as weak, irresponsible, immature, unwise, or think of us as a burden in some way.

The reality is that more than half of the time, these feelings are almost never based on our past experiences but are often purely based on our own assumptions about how we expect things will turn out. This problem is an exaggerated characteristic in those of us suffering from imposter syndrome because us 'imposters' are already victims of severe anxiety, personal feelings of incompetence, self-doubt, and fear of failure (this includes the fear of rejection and fear of being perceived as a failure by someone else). We are therefore twice as likely to avoid asking for help (even when they really need it) or are more likely to have trouble communicating our feelings and emotions properly during situations of high pressure/stress.

Using Dr. Valerie Young's description of the different types of imposters, it can be seen that each type will struggle to ask for help, or struggle to communicate their problems effectively based on their unique characteristics. For example, a 'perfectionist' might have trouble delegating because they do not trust others to do things as perfectly as they would. The 'superhero' might have trouble accepting help because it takes away from their ability to feel 'useful' and 'needed'. The 'natural genius' might feel like asking for help confirms their suspicions that they aren't as inherently capable as what is being perceived by others. The 'expert' may struggle to ask for help in situations that relate to their area of expertise, fearing that people may perceive them as either 'unskilled' or 'a fraud'. The 'rugged individualist' may fear that asking for help invalidates their contribution towards their achievement by transferring all the credit to the helper.

The tendency for 'imposters' to reject help in critical situations can lead to feelings of isolation, and it can also make already tough situations even more challenging to manage. Although it's true that there are a wide variety of self-help information and activities available for the average 'imposter', more likely than not, they will eventually reach a mental plateau. This seemingly 'unbreakable barrier' occurs because further development of our own self-awareness has become virtually impossible without the help of others. In other words, without communication, help and support from others, we are unable to reconcile the disconnect that exists between how we perceive ourselves and how others perceive us.

One important way for us 'imposters' to break our limiting beliefs is by allowing ourselves to open up to new experiences, information, and perspectives. Seeking social support is an excellent way to achieve this, since it provides us with a much-needed change in outlook about our experiences. It can also provide us with the encouragement and the energy that we need to keep going.

In summary, asking for help can benefit 'imposters' in five important ways. These are:

- It helps us to build and maintain connections/relationships with others.
- It can provide us with new ideas and a change in outlook/perspective.
- It helps us to avoid mental exhaustion/burnout by giving us an opportunity to discuss/work through our problems.
- It helps us to achieve our goals faster than if we did them alone.
- It helps us to build confidence both in ourselves and in others.

Regardless of how we feel about receiving assistance versus providing it, the general consensus is that asking for support is a strength and not a weakness. And deep down somewhere, most of us know this (at least in theory). However, for a lot of us the problem might not be our willingness to ask for help, but sometimes we might simply be unsure about how to go about asking for the help we need the right way.

Perhaps we let the situation go on for too long before seeking out assistance, so our feelings have escalated to the point where we can't communicate as coherently as we would like.

Or perhaps we did communicate with someone before it was too late, but in retrospect we realized that we didn't quite say everything we wanted to say (maybe we didn't remember to include an important topic because we were just 'winging' the conversation).

SAMPLE EXERCISE 7 – A REVIEW OF HOW AND WHY WE ASK FOR SUPPORT

The art of asking for help is actually a very underrated skill that we could all use some guidance on. Let's assess/evaluate our capacity to ask for assistance/support by continuing with Daniel's example, which was provided in sample exercise 6.1.

1. Describe the situation that you may need assistance/ guidance/ support to resolve. Why are you seeking help in this instance?

Daniel's Answer: *"I had an argument with my wife where I expressed my anger physically. I am concerned that my issues with communication are negatively affecting my marriage."*

2. Describe the emotions that you are currently experiencing because of the above situation.

Daniel's Answer: *"I have feelings of shame, regret, worry, anxiety, and sadness about what happened."*

3. Who do you think would be the best person to discuss the problem with?

( ) A relative/family
( ) A neighbor
(X) A friend
( ) A work colleague
( ) A stranger
( ) A licensed professional

4. Why did you select this person as your first choice when seeking assistance or support in this situation?

Daniel's Answer: *"Steve has been my best friend for almost 15 years, and I trust him more than anyone I know. He has been married to his wife for 10 years and I really respect and admire how gently and thoughtfully he communicates with her."*

5. When do you think is the best time to ask this person for assistance or support?

Daniel's Answer: *"I think the best time to ask him about the situation is next Saturday while we are having a beer and watching a football game."*

6. Do you have any concerns over how you will be perceived when you ask for assistance/support from this person? If you do, what are these concerns?

Daniel's Answer: *"I feel like Steve might think that I am some kind of abusive person, even though I have not and would never lay a hand on my wife."*

7. Do you believe that the person you have selected for assistance or support may reject your request? Why or why not?

Daniel's Answer: *"I have a nagging suspicion that talking about my marriage might make him uncomfortable, since he doesn't always like to talk about personal matters."*

8. What are your goals or expectations for the outcome of your request/discussion with this person?

Daniel's Answer: *"I would like him to give me some insight on how he communicates in his marriage. For example, how he manages to find the resolve to speak candidly/openly with his wife, and how he deals with not taking things too personally when his wife speaks candidly/openly with him."*

9. Do you think that asking for assistance or support will bring you closer to your goals?

Daniel's Answer: *"Indeed, I do. Without support, I'm afraid that I will make the same old foolish mistakes until finally, it's too late. I need an objective opinion about my behavior and my current capacity* *for communication. I think that talking to my best friend will point me in the right direction."*

10. What do you think you would be sacrificing by asking for help in this situation?

Daniel's Answer: *"My pride as a man, and as an independent man at that. Plus, I'm 3 years older than Steve, so I might also lose his respect if I ask his advice on this."*

11. What do you think you would be sacrificing by avoiding asking for help in this situation?

Daniel's Answer: *"My marriage and my happiness."*

12. If your request for assistance or support is rejected, what do you think should be your next step?

Daniel's Answer: *"My marriage is very important to me, so if Steve says no, I will talk to my dad about it. He's a bit old fashioned, but maybe he might be able to help me figure out what I'm missing."*

13. After reviewing all that you have stated thus far, do you believe that the 'benefits' associated with seeking assistance or support in this situation outweigh the 'risks'? Why?

Daniel's Answer: *"Yes, I do. I would rather do everything I can to protect my marriage, than let our years of hard work go down the drain because of my crass methods of communicating. I recognize that Steve could say no, or possibly judge me for it, but that is a risk that I am willing to take given the situation."*

EXERCISE 7 – A REVIEW OF HOW AND WHY WE ASK FOR SUPPORT

Let's assess/evaluate our capacity to ask for assistance/support by answering the following questions:

Describe the situation that you may need assistance/ guidance/ support to resolve. Why are you seeking help in this instance?

_____

_____

_____

_____

_____

_____

_____

_____

Describe the emotions that you are currently experiencing because of the above situation.

_____

_____

_____

_____

_____

_____

_____

_____

Who do you think would be the best person to discuss the problem with?

( ) A relative/family
( ) A neighbor
( ) A friend
( ) A work colleague
( ) A stranger
( ) A licensed professional

Why did you select this person as your first choice when seeking assistance or support in this situation?

_____

_____

_____

_____

_____

_____

When do you think is the best time to ask this person for assistance or support?

_____

_____

_____

_____

_____

_____

Do you have any concerns over how you will be perceived when you ask for assistance or support from this person? If you do, what are these concerns?

_____

_____

_____

_____

_____

_____

_____

_____

_____

_____

Do you believe that the person you have selected for assistance or support may reject your request? Why or why not?

_____

_____

_____

_____

_____

_____

_____

_____

_____

_____

What are your goals or expectations for the outcome of your request/discussion with this person?

_____

_____

_____

_____

_____

_____

_____

_____

_____

_____

Do you think that asking for assistance or support will bring you closer to your goals?

_____

_____

_____

_____

_____

_____

_____

_____

_____

_____

What do you think you would be sacrificing by asking for help in this situation?

_____

_____

_____

_____

_____

_____

_____

_____

_____

_____

What do you think you would be sacrificing by avoiding asking for help in this situation?

_____

_____

_____

_____

_____

_____

_____

_____

_____

_____

If your request for assistance or support is rejected, what do you think should be your next step?

_____

_____

_____

_____

_____

_____

_____

_____

_____

_____

After reviewing all that you have stated thus far, do you believe that the 'benefits' associated with seeking assistance or support in this situation outweigh the 'risks'? Why?

_____

_____

_____

_____

_____

_____

_____

_____

_____

_____

Chapter 8

BUILDING SELF-ESTEEM AND SELF-CONFIDENCE

S elf-confidence is defined as our ability to trust our own qualities, skills, and judgement. Of course, this belief in ourselves has nothing to do with our actual ability to complete a task successfully. It refers to the level of trust that we have in ourselves about our capacity to succeed at any task that we set our mind to do. The ability of some people to exude more self-confidence than others during specific situation is not based on any innate attributes, such as genetics. It is something that we develop over time, and it is based on our experiences (knowledge and practice), as well as how we value ourselves as a result of those experiences (also known as our self-esteem). Self-confidence (our ability to trust our own capabilities), and self-esteem (our ability to value ourselves) are indeed not one and the same. However, our ability to value ourselves directly affects our ability to trust our own capabilities, which means that to build our self-confidence, we must first work on building our self-esteem.

Self-esteem is deeply rooted in or sense of identity, and it is usually developed during our childhood years. Abuse (both verbal and physical), neglect, discrimination, excessive criticism, and lack of affection during childhood are all potential causes for the development of low self-esteem later on in life. In addition, low self-esteem is not a fixed trait, but it can fluctuate in frequency and intensity during different circumstances in our lives. This means that the emotions that are generally associated with having low self-esteem, such as feelings of worthlessness, hopelessness, and self-hate, all fluctuate.

Signs of low self-esteem typically include:

- Feeling unloved, or undeserving of love.
- Having an excessive amount of negative self-talk.
- Highlighting our negative attributes and downplaying our positive attributes.
- Blaming ourselves for mistakes and situations that are out of our control.
- Doubting others when they give us a compliment.
- Avoiding taking credit for our achievements and successes.

Having a problem with low self-esteem is also a direct precursor to developing low self-confidence and depression. A lack of self-confidence means that our negative internal self-talk is the main driving force that controls our decisions and actions. If we have low self-confidence, we aren't as likely to set challenging goals for ourselves or achieve the goals that we have set for ourselves. We are also more likely to experience difficulties in our personal and professional relationships due to the social anxiety that can often accompany low self-confidence.

Signs of low self-confidence include:

- Doubting our decisions and actions.
- Avoiding taking the lead and generally being passive/submissive.
- Not trusting others to help and support us.

- Having feelings of interiority when comparing ourselves to others.
- Being unable to handle criticism.
- Avoiding trying new or challenging experiences.

Unfortunately, us 'imposters' are stuck in a never-ending cycle where our low self-esteem feeds into our low self-confidence , and our low self-confidence puts us into negative situations that feed back into our low self-esteem. However, this cycle can be broken by increasing our self-awareness, exercising self-compassion, celebrating our small wins, showing gratitude often and practicing daily affirmations.

EXERCISE 8.1 – ASSESSING YOUR LEVEL OF SELF-CONFIDENCE AND GENERAL APPROACH TO LIFE

Let's get started by assessing your level of self-confidence. Circle your personal response that is most true for each statement.

Statements	Responses				
	Strongly Agree	**Agree**	**Neutral**	**Disagree**	**Strongly Disagree**
I am fully aware of my strengths and weaknesses.	1	2	3	4	5
I am open to take chances on anything that I believe in.	1	2	3	4	5
I often reflect on my past wins as a form of encouragement and motivation.	1	2	3	4	5
I fully acknowledge that failure is just another part of my life experience.	1	2	3	4	5
I am not afraid to ask for assistance or support when I need it.	1	2	3	4	5
I believe that my actions align with my values.	1	2	3	4	5
I am persistent when it comes to achieving any task that I set my mind to do.	1	2	3	4	5

I understand and acknowledge that everyone may not like or accept me for who I am.	1	2	3	4	5
I believe that my self-worth is not tied to my successes or failures.	1	2	3	4	5
I can face any challenges and unexpected situations that I may encounter.	1	2	3	4	5
I do not hesitate when it comes to trying something new.	1	2	3	4	5
I practice self-compassion when I am going through a significantly negative experience.	1	2	3	4	5
I can cope with rejection and criticism.	1	2	3	4	5
I see failure as just another learning experience.	1	2	3	4	5
I feel proud when I have an opportunity to demonstrate my knowledge and skills to others.	1	2	3	4	5

If you have a score of 40 or less, you exude confidence and you do not let obstacles stop you from achieving your goals.

If you have a score of between 41 and 60, you are mostly confident during situations where you feel like you are right in your comfort zone. You may suffer from periods of low self-confidence when you experience moderate to severe failures, but you generally bounce back after a while.

If you have a score over 60, you are not confident in your power and abilities to affect your surroundings or circumstances. You may frequently experience some of the common traits associated with low self-confidence, which includes anxiety, depression, and low self-esteem.

SAMPLE EXERCISE 8.2 – IDENTIFYING AND INTERNALIZING YOUR STRENGTHS AND WEAKNESSES

For this exercise, you are going to create a customized inventory of some potential attributes that support your internal view of self, as well as your external view of how you relate to others. You will then extract items that you consider to be weaknesses and strengths, and revise them according to the criteria that we will cover a bit later. Start by listing positive attributes (strengths) with a '+', and negative attributes (weaknesses) with a '-'.

In this example, Erica has listed her strengths and weaknesses for each category as follows:

Body Image and Appearance

Things you can consider including in this category are your facial appearance, weight, height, complexion, and other descriptions that relate to your physical body and appearance.

Erica listed:

+ Big blue eyes	- Ugly nose
+ Long blonde hair	- Short neck
+ Youthful looking skin (no pimples)	+ No need to use make-up
- Crooked teeth	- Looks terrible in dresses
- Belly fat	- Has chin hair
- Small breasts	- Short

Interaction/Communication with Other People

Include descriptions of how you relate to family, friends. strangers and coworkers in social situations.

Erica listed:

+ Playful with kids   + Tolerant and accepting of people

- Shy with strangers   + Willing to compromise

- Insincere with coworkers   - Secretive

+ Good at listening   - Manipulative

- Not good at asking for help   + Dependable

How I See Myself

Include all of your personality traits that come to mind, both positive and negative.

Erica listed:

+ Responsible   - Fickle

+ Caring   + Dedicated

+ Industrious   + Honest

- Jealous   - Introverted

- Too Sensitive   - Moody

How I Think That Others See Me

Things you can consider including in this category are positive and negative traits that your family and friends see/comment on.

Erica listed:

- Spiteful   - Quirky

- Forgetful   - Broody

+ Warm   + Forgiving

+ Easygoing   - Too strict

+ Productive

Work and/or Academic Performance

Describe how you handle your daily obligations at work and at school.

Erica listed:

+ Meticulous   - Never contacts clients via telephone

+ Reliable   - Not a team player

+ Good at follow-up   + Pleasant

- Easily stressed   + Professional

- Prone to panic   - Avoid making presentations

Daily Life/Task Performance

Describe how you maintain your living space, what you do in terms of self-care, and how you generally take care of the needs of your family.

Erica listed:

- Prone to overspending   - Always fussing about my appearance

- Never cleans the house   - Always forgets the mail in the mailbox

+ Always remember appointments   - Overeats

+ Always pays bills on time   + Picks up nephew from daycare

+ Good cook

General Mental Well-Being

Things you can consider including in this category are your problem-solving capabilities, your ability to reason, be creative, be insightful and so on.

Erica listed:

+ Highly Attentive   - Bad at debating

+ Curious   - Not very imaginative

+ Logical thinker   - Experiences mental fatigue easily

- Slow learner   - Stubborn

Now that you have listed your positive and negative attributes, extract the negative attributes and place them in the table that we have provided below. Let's focus on each weakness and revise them according to the following criteria:

- Avoid using harsh, critical language that can be interpreted as judgmental or destructive. For example:

  1) "Ugly nose" can be changed to say, "I have a prominent nose".

  2) "Manipulative" can be changed to say, "I am committed to achieving a particular outcome and will often do so through micromanaging."

  3) "Often neglects to clean the house" can be reworded to say, "I frequently overwork myself to the point of exhaustion, and I often just go straight to bed when I get home, which leaves no time for housework."

- Therefore, the aim is to eliminate all words that have negative undertones, such as "fat", "terrible", "insincere", "moody", and so on. These negative words may seem inert when viewed in insolation, but they are the exact same words that we experience internally as negative self-talk. The sooner you can identify these words and rid them from your vocabulary, the better.

- Try to be accurate with your descriptions and be specific in the language that you use to describe yourself. Most of us tend to exaggerate our negative traits, however, the goal is to be able to describe ourselves as objectively as possible. For example:

  1) The phrase "crooked teeth" is both inaccurate and very critical. A more objective, factual description would be "I have two misaligned top lateral incisors due to removing my braces too early."

  2) The phrase "insincere with coworkers" is also very negative and embellished. A more accurate description would be "My anxiety and social awkwardness causes me to miss certain

social cues and this is more pronounced with acquaintances and strangers."

- Wherever applicable, start the description by listing the corresponding strength. For example, instead of saying "I experience mental fatigue easily", Erica could choose to say "I am focused and alert when I can complete my tasks in a planned, orderly manner. But the minute things become chaotic, I feel drained because my attention is too divided."

Let's review Erica's revised list of negative attributes:

Original Attribute Descriptions	Revised Attribute Descriptions

1. Body Image and Appearance

Crooked teeth	I have two misaligned top lateral incisors due to removing my braces too early.
Belly fat	I have a 49-inch waist.
Small breasts	I have a petite chest size, which suits my delicate frame.
Ugly nose	I have a prominent nose.
Short neck	My neck and shoulders are strong and sturdy.
Looks terrible in dresses	Dresses flatter my figure and give me a soft and feminine appeal, but I prefer a powerful and assertive appearance.
Has chin hair	I have endometriosis, which causes four to five single hairs to grow on my chin every six to eight weeks.
Short	I am 5 feet, 3 inches tall.

2. Interaction/Communication with Other People

Shy with strangers	I find it easier to start conversations with people I know personally. I can sometimes hesitate when starting a conversation with someone I haven't met before.
Insincere with coworkers	My anxiety and social awkwardness cause me to miss certain social cues, and this is more pronounced with acquaintances and strangers.
Not good at asking for help	I get nervous when asking my coworkers to demonstrate new tasks or to cover for me when I take my lunch break.

Secretive

I am a very private person, which makes people get very curious about my private life. My desire for privacy causes me to be very careful with how I act in public and to be very selective with the information that I share.

Manipulative

I am committed to achieving a particular outcome and will often do so through micromanaging.

3. How I See Myself

Jealous

I do not like to share, and I am a bit possessive when it comes to money and relationships.

Sensitive

I am in tune with my emotions.

Fickle

I find staying at home to be relaxing and comforting. As a result, I usually cancel at the last minute whenever I agree to plans with friends and coworkers.

Introvert

Interacting with people drains my energy rather quickly. Therefore, I prefer solitary activities that allow me to conserve and/or replenish my energy.

Moody

I believe that I should have the freedom to change my mind whenever I want, and I exercise this freedom fairly frequently.

4. How I Think That Others See Me

Spiteful

I can sometimes find it hard to forgive the people who have wronged me, but I eventually end up forgiving the person and moving on.

Forgetful

I often have so many work tasks on my to-do list that I might forget other, less important tasks. Like doing the laundry or watering my plants.

Quirky	I am very unique.
Broody	When a situation happens that I do not understand, I relive it over and over again in my mind until I can make sense of what happened.
Too Strict	When it comes to my job, I am very rigid about my routine and my obligations. Because of this, my coworkers might occasionally complain about my inflexibility.

5. Work and/or Academic Performance

Easily stressed	When work processes are not done in an organized way, I tend to get scatter-brained and irritable.
Prone to panic	I find it difficult to handle sudden changes and unforeseen situations.
Never contacts clients via telephone	I am not a strong verbal communicator. Therefore, I focus my attention on other more passive forms of communication, such as emails.
Not a team player	I prefer to do things alone because it means that I can achieve my desired outcome.
Avoid making presentations	I can handle presenting to small groups of familiar people, but I struggle when the people I am presenting to are strangers, or if it is a large group of people.

6. Daily Life/Task Performance

Prone to overspending	I find making new purchases to be therapeutic, but I often go over budget.
Never cleans the house	I frequently overwork myself to the point of exhaustion. I just go straight to bed when I get home, which leaves no time for housework.

Always fussing about my appearance	I spend an extra 15 minutes in the mirror each morning taming stray hairs, checking for lint and adjusting my blouses to fit properly.
Always forgets the mail in the mailbox	I consider collecting the mail to be a low-priority task.
Overeats	I use eating as a way to comfort myself whenever I've had a stressful day.

7. General Mental Well-Being

Slow learner	I need to read through new material quite a few times to retain the information.
Bad at debating	My lack of assertiveness causes me to be submissive during heated discussions.
Not very imaginative	I prefer non-fictional information and I find it hard to relate to concepts that have a highly imaginative component.
Experiences mental fatigue easily	I am focused and alert when I can complete my planned tasks in an orderly manner. But the minute things become chaotic, I feel drained since my attention is too divided.
Stubborn	When I set my mind to something, it takes a significant amount of convincing for me to change it.

Erica has chosen to revise a few of her positive attributes as well. Let's review Erica's revised list below:

Original Attribute Descriptions	**Revised Attribute Descriptions**
1. Body Image and Appearance	
Big blue eyes	My blue eyes are the most striking feature on my face.
Long blonde hair	I have thick, healthy, blonde hair, that I have allowed to grow to waist length.
Youthful looking skin (no pimples)	I have smooth skin and no wrinkles or large pores.
No need to use make-up	I only need to apply sunscreen and a lip moisturizer to appear 'put together'.
2. Interaction/Communication with Other People	
Playful with kids	I love to interact with kids because I find it easy to be myself around them. This makes me look forward to spending time with the kids in my family, such as my nephew.
Good at listening	I am generally receptive and a good listener when communicating with people because it gives me an opportunity to learn a bit about them.
Tolerant and accepting	I am very liberal with my views, and I am usually willing to accept the social and cultural differences between me and other people.
Willing to compromise	I am willing to meet others halfway because I do not like confrontation.
Dependable	I really appreciate reliable people. I try to be reliable because it aligns with my values.

3. How I See Myself

Caring
    I am gentle and affectionate with close friends and family.

Industrious
    I am a hard worker when it comes to my career and academic pursuits.

Dedicated
    I am loyal when it comes to the things that I believe in.

Honest
    I tell the truth most of the time.

4. How I Think That Others See Me

Warm
    I am very affectionate to my sisters and grandparents.

Forgiving
    I generally forgive friends and family more quickly than acquaintances and strangers.

5. Work and/or Academic Performance

Professional
    I never mix work with my personal life.

6. Daily Life/Task Performance

Always remember my appointments
    I place high-priority tasks in a task management app so that I will not forget the dates and times of important events.

Always pays bills on time
    I have a strong sense of responsibility when it comes to civil obligations.

Good cook
    My family enjoys the food I make.

7. General Mental Well-Being

Curious
    I actively research topics that interest me.

Logical
    I use reason and rational thinking as my main tools of understanding the external world.

Review your positive and negative attributes one more time. Focus on making the description of each attribute a complete sentence. Add adjectives, synonyms, and adverbs wherever necessary.

Now it's time to write a self-description based on your revised positive and negative attribute descriptions only. Let's see what Erica has to say:

I am 5 feet 3 inches tall, with striking blue eyes, a prominent nose, and long, thick, healthy blonde hair. I have a 49-inch waist, and a petite chest size, which suits my delicate frame. My neck and shoulders are strong and sturdy, and I have two misaligned incisors because my braces were removed too early. My skin is smooth, and I only need to apply sunscreen and lip moisturizer to appear 'put together'. Dresses flatter my figure and give me a soft and feminine appeal, but I prefer a powerful and assertive appearance. I have endometriosis, which causes four to five single hairs to grow on my chin every six to eight weeks.

My anxiety and social awkwardness cause me to miss certain social cues, but I am very receptive and a good listener when communicating with people. I find it easier to start conversations with people I know personally and can sometimes hesitate when starting a conversation with someone I haven't met before. However, I love to interact and be playful with kids. I really appreciate reliable people, and I am willing to meet others halfway because I do not like confrontation. I am very liberal with my views, but I am also a very private person. I am committed to achieving a particular outcome and will often do so through micromanaging. I get nervous when asking my coworkers to demonstrate new tasks or to cover for me when I take my lunch break.

I am gentle and affectionate with close friends and family, and I am loyal when it comes to the things that I believe in. I am in tune with my emotions, and I tell the truth most of the time. I believe that I should have the freedom to change my mind whenever I want, and I exercise this right regularly. I do not like to share, and I am a bit possessive when it comes to money and relationships. Interacting with people drains my energy, so I frequently cancel plans with friends and coworkers at the last minute. I am a hard worker when it comes to my career and academic pursuits.

I am very affectionate to my sisters and grandparents. I generally forgive friends and family more quickly than acquaintances and strangers. When it comes to my job, I am very rigid about my routine and my obligations. If a situation happens that I do not understand, I tend to replay it over and over again in my mind until I can make sense of what happened. I often have so many work tasks on my to-do list that I tend to forget other less important tasks, like doing the laundry or watering my plants.

I never mix work with my personal life. When work processes are not done in an organized way, I tend to get scatter-brained and irritable. I find it difficult to handle sudden changes and unforeseen situations. I prefer to do things alone because it means that I can achieve my desired outcome. I am not a strong verbal communicator, therefore, I focus my attention on other more passive forms of communication, such as sending emails. I can handle presenting to small groups of familiar people, but I struggle if the group I am presenting to are strangers, or if it is a large group of people.

I frequently overwork myself to the point of exhaustion. I often just go straight to bed when I get home, which leaves no time for housework. I use eating as a way to comfort myself whenever I've had a stressful day. I also find shopping to be therapeutic, but I often go over budget. I spend an extra 15 minutes in the mirror each morning taming stray hairs, checking for lint and adjusting my blouses to fit properly. I have a strong sense of responsibility when it comes to civil obligations. I place high-priority tasks in a task management app so that I will not forget the dates and times of important events. I consider collecting the mail to be a low-priority task.

I use reason and rational thinking as my main tools of understanding the external world. I prefer non-fictional information and I find it hard to relate to concepts that have a highly imaginative component. I actively research topics that interest me. I need to read through new material quite a few times to retain the information. When I set my mind to something, it takes a significant amount of convincing for me to change it.

EXERCISE 8.2 – IDENTIFYING AND INTERNALIZING YOUR STRENGTHS AND WEAKNESSES

For this exercise, you are going to create a customized inventory of some potential attributes that support your internal view of self, as well as your external view of how you relate to others. You will then extract items that you consider to be weaknesses and strengths and revise them according to the criteria that we will cover a bit later. Start by listing positive attributes (strengths) with a '+', and negative attributes (weaknesses) with a '-'.

Body Image and Appearance

Things you can consider including in this category are your facial appearance, weight, height, complexion, and other descriptions that relate to your physical body and appearance.

Your list:

_____   _____

_____   _____

_____   _____

_____   _____

_____   _____

_____   _____

Interaction/Communication with Other People

Include descriptions of how you relate to family, friends. strangers and coworkers in social situations.

Your list:

_____ _____

_____ _____

_____ _____

_____ _____

_____ _____

_____ _____

How I See Myself

Include all of your personality traits that come to mind, both positive and negative.

_____ _____

_____ _____

_____ _____

_____ _____

_____ _____

_____ _____

How I Think That Others See Me

Things you can consider including in this category are positive and negative traits that your family and friends see/comment on.

Your list:

_____   _____

_____   _____

_____   _____

_____   _____

_____   _____

_____   _____

Work and/or Academic Performance

Describe how you handle your daily obligations at work and at school.

Your list:

_____   _____

_____   _____

_____   _____

_____   _____

_____   _____

_____   _____

Daily Life/Task Performance

Describe how you maintain your living space, what you do in terms of self-care, and how you generally take care of the needs of your family.

Your list:

_____   _____

_____   _____

_____   _____

_____   _____

_____   _____

General Mental Well-Being

Things you can consider including in this category are your problem-solving capabilities, your ability to reason, be creative, be insightful and so on.

Your list:

_____   _____

_____   _____

_____   _____

_____   _____

_____   _____

Now that you have listed your positive and negative attributes, extract the negative attributes and place them in the table that we have provided. Remember to focus on each weakness and revise them according to the following criteria:

- Avoid using harsh, critical language that can be interpreted as judgmental or destructive.
- Try to be accurate with your descriptions and be specific in the language that you use to describe yourself.
- Wherever applicable, start the description by listing the corresponding strength.

Let's revise your top 5 negative attributes:

Original Attribute Descriptions	Revised Attribute Descriptions
1. Body Image and Appearance	

Original Attribute Descriptions	Revised Attribute Descriptions
2. Interaction/Communication with Other People	

Original Attribute Descriptions	Revised Attribute Descriptions
3. How I See Myself	

Original Attribute Descriptions	Revised Attribute Descriptions
4. How I Think That Others See Me	

Original Attribute Descriptions	Revised Attribute Descriptions
5. Work and/or Academic Performance	

Original Attribute Descriptions	Revised Attribute Descriptions
6. Daily Life/Task Performance	

Original Attribute Descriptions	Revised Attribute Descriptions
7. General Mental Well-Being	

Let's revise your top 5 positive attributes:

Original Attribute Descriptions	Revised Attribute Descriptions
1. Body Image and Appearance	

Original Attribute Descriptions	Revised Attribute Descriptions
2. Interaction/Communication with Other People	

Original Attribute Descriptions	Revised Attribute Descriptions
3. How I See Myself	

Original Attribute Descriptions	Revised Attribute Descriptions
4. How I Think That Others See Me	

Original Attribute Descriptions	Revised Attribute Descriptions
5. Work and/or Academic Performance	

Original Attribute Descriptions	Revised Attribute Descriptions
6. Daily Life/Task Performance	

Original Attribute Descriptions	Revised Attribute Descriptions
7. General Mental Well-Being	

Review your positive and negative attributes one more time. Focus on making the description of each attribute a complete sentence. Add adjectives, synonyms, and adverbs wherever necessary. Now it's time to write a self-description based on your revised positive and negative attribute descriptions only:

_____

_____

_____

_____

_____

_____

_____

_____

_____

_____

_____

_____

_____

_____

_____

_____

_____

_____

_____

_____

_____

_____

Chapter 9

TAKING ACTION AND
MAKING CHANGES

We have all made at least one New Year's Eve resolution with utmost sincerity and conviction, only to later get distracted by the events of daily life. Or some of us may have started working towards our goals only to slowly lose motivation over time. The reasons behind our failure to follow-through with the goals that we have set can range from insufficient planning, selecting goals that are too vague, the occurrence of unanticipated events (such as sickness, legal matters, and economic recessions), or just good old procrastination. All of us have been affected by one or more of these issues, some more than others. But there is one more important reason why us 'imposters' fail to invest enough effort to reach our goals. This reason is: we are inclined to set unrealistic goals, since most of us hold ourselves to unattainable standards.

Unrealistic goals are goals that are difficult to attain because we do not have the time, energy, resources or the relevant skills required to see them through to fruition. Unattainable standards are a set of unrealistically high expectations that we place on ourselves. These expectations may be very difficult to fulfill (for example, a student who expects to always have A+ grades, despite not having received many A+'s in the past). Or these expectations can be entirely impossible to fulfill (for example, an overweight person who wants to lose 200 pounds by dieting for 7 days). We set these unrealistic standards and goals for ourselves in a futile attempt to finally be considered as worthy of our achievements. When we undoubtedly fail to meet our own expectations, we experience negative feelings, we fixate on the disappointment, and we make inaccurate conclusions. Then, we think and act in ways that feed into an endless cycle of failures and disappointments.

If we set goals that are realistic and that support our personal values, then the biggest secret to achieving these goals is vested in one thing only, effort. However, taking the necessary action to achieve our goals and make positive changes in or lives is not as straightforward as it seems. One major reason for this is the tendency for human beings to place a higher value on smaller, immediate rewards versus bigger, more long-term rewards. That is, when it comes to deciding which action we should take in the moment, we are more likely to prefer the choice that gives us instant gratification, even if it is to the detriment of our future self. This concept is actually referred to as 'present bias', and it is a theory which was developed by US economist and behavioral psychologist Richard Thaler.

Present bias suggests that when we decide on a goal, like for example, learning a new language or losing a few pounds, the plans that we make to achieve that goal are actually for our future self, not our present self. During the goal setting process, our brains can easily envision how wonderful we will feel in the future to have taken the necessary actions to achieve our desired goal. However, when it is time to actually execute the steps that we had previously envisioned, this is no longer a decision for our future self, now it becomes a decision for our present self. Suddenly, we realize that completing the planned action will not give us any immediate benefits, so we decide to complete another unrelated action that gives us instant gratification instead. For example, perhaps before going to bed we resolve that we want to lose 15 pounds, and that we want to achieve this by jogging for 30 minutes every morning. Of course, this means that we need to wake up 30 minutes earlier than normal, so we eagerly set our alarm for 4:30am instead of the usual 5:00am. In the morning, the alarm goes off at 4:30am, and our present self is faced with two decisions: get up and go for a jog or press snooze for 5 minutes. At this point, our present self might not see the immediate benefits of getting up, putting on our sweatpants, going outside in the cold and jogging diligently until we are sweaty and tired. We will, however, see the immediate benefits of getting 5 minutes more sleep.

Learning to resist the allure of instant gratification is not easy to do, but it will help us to bridge the gap between the decisions made by our present self and our future self. Let's review a few ways that this can be achieved.

Use a 'Commitment Device' When Making Future Plans

A commitment device is a decision made by our present self that intentionally binds our future self to complete the desired action. When our decisions incorporate a commitment device, we attach a cost to not completing the desired action.

For example, suppose instead we told a friend about our goal of losing a few pounds and we made plans to wake up 30 minutes earlier to go jogging with that friend. Our friend would be upset that we stood them up if we didn't meet up with them to exercise at the scheduled time. Therefore, there is a social cost to not completing the action that we have planned for our future self.

Another example would be if we made plans to lose those 15 pounds by controlling our portion sizes and eating healthy food. If we threw out all of our larger sized lunchbox containers and replaced them with smaller ones, we are more likely to stick to our meal plan. The costs of not sticking to our meal prep would be the hassle of finding a replacement lunch (and there will also be a financial cost attached too!).

Incorporate 'Implementation Intention' in Your Action Plans

An implementation intention essentially outlines how, when and where the specific actions should be used in order to achieve the specific goals that we have set for ourselves. In order to execute implementation intention, we must describe the precise action that we want to complete, then add the specific time and location that we would like to complete the action. For example:

Goal: I want to lose 15 pounds.

Implementation Intention:
How: I will exercise on the treadmill for 45 minutes every morning before work
When: from 4:15am to 5:00am
Where: at my neighborhood gym

Goal: I want to learn to speak French.

Implementation Intention:
How: I will practice the French language learning activities every Monday, Wednesday, and Friday
When: from 2:00pm to 3:00pm
Where: on the Duolingo app

The implementation intention aspect of planning out our goals removes the need for our future selves to make decisions, thus increasing the likelihood that we will actually follow through with the actions that we have planned.

Make it Easier to Start the Desired Action

For many of us, taking the very first step towards a goal can be the hardest part of any plan. For us 'imposters', overthinking, self-doubt, and fear of failure might be the reasons we procrastinate when it comes to actually initiating the positive actions that can have beneficial, liberating, and transformational effects on our lives. The best way to reduce the friction experienced when starting a desired action is to break the task down into a series of manageable micro-actions.

For example, if your goal is to improve your self-care routine in order to help boost your self-confidence, then you may want to take actions such as (for example) buying new clothes, grooming your hair, doing yoga, and taking better care of your skin and appearance. If you suffer from imposter syndrome, the action of 'buying new clothes' might actually be quite overwhelming. "Where would I purchase these clothes from?" "How will I know what is fashionable and what suits me?" "What if I gain weight, would I still be able to fit the clothes I buy today?" You can easily overthink yourself into being paralyzed with inaction. Then it becomes all too easy to just put off the action of buying new clothes until next week.

However, if you divide the action of buying new clothes into several micro-actions, then it might become easier to start and complete your desired action. For example, you can write out a list of small actions that you could take over the first two weeks as follows:

Saturday Morning (Week 1)

- Browse through women's tops on Amazon.com for 20-30 minutes
- Buy one white blouse (large)

Saturday Morning (Week 2)

- Visit Macy's department store for 30-40 minutes
- Buy one pair of black slacks (1x)
- Buy one pair of blue jeans (1x)

SAMPLE EXERCISE 9 – SETTING GOALS AND TAKING ACTIONS TO ACHIEVE THEM

Step 1: *Decide on one of the following life areas that you would like to work on:*

Daniel's Answer:

( ) Career
( ) Family
( ) Health
( ) Social
(**X**) Financial
( ) Personal Development
( ) Education
( ) Travel

Step 2: *Write down three goals that you would like to achieve within the life area that you have selected (be sure to rank them by order of priority/importance):*

Daniel's Answer:

Goal #1: Accumulate $20,000 in savings within the next 12 months.
Goal #2: Pay off credit card next month ($2,000).
Goal #3: Start a new business in the venture capital market.

Step 3: *Describe the first three actions that you will need to take to achieve your selected goal.*

Daniel's Answer:

    Goal #1: Accumulate $20,000 in savings within the next 12 months.

1.   Avoid overspending on clothes and gadgets.
2.   Restrict grocery spending to $800 - $900 a month.
3.   Deposit $450 in a joint savings account every week.

Step 4: *Break down each action into a series of micro-actions. For example, for Action #2 (restrict grocery spending to $800 - $900 a month), Daniel has planned out the following micro-actions:*

Micro Actions	Behavior	When		Where
1	Check kitchen every day to select and use up short shelf-life ingredients before they expire (to reduce wastage).	6:10am 6:15am	to	The kitchen
2	Make a weekly grocery list of only necessary items every Saturday ($200 - $225 spending limit).	7:30am 7:45am	to	On living room sofa
3	Swap expensive items with cheaper substitutes (laundry detergent and frozen foods) when grocery shopping every week.	11:00am 12:30pm	to	Costco

The Imposter Syndrome Workbook

Step 5: *Track your progress over the next 8 weeks to see how well you have been putting your goals into action. Here are Daniel's results for Week 1:*

Week 1

List of Weekly Actions	Mond	Tuesd	Wednesd	Thursd	Frida	Saturda	Sund
Check kitchen every day to select and use up short shelf-life ingredients .	1	1	2			1	
Make a weekly grocery list of only necessary items every Saturday .						1	
Swap expensive items with cheaper substitutes (laundry detergent and frozen foods) when						1	
Use coupons daily for breakfast cereals, pastries, and coffee.		2	1	3			

EXERCISE 9 – SETTING GOALS AND TAKING ACTIONS TO ACHIEVE THEM

Step 1: *Decide on one of the following life areas that you would like to work on:*

( ) Career
( ) Family
( ) Health
( ) Social
( ) Financial
( ) Personal Development
( ) Education
( ) Travel

Step 2: *Write down three goals that you would like to achieve within the life area that you have selected (be sure to rank them by order of priority/importance):*

Goal #1: _____

_____

_____

Goal #2: _____

_____

_____

Goal #3: _____

_____

_____

Step 3: *Describe the first three actions that you will need to take to achieve your selected goal.*

Goal: _____

_____

Action 1. _____

_____

_____

_____

Action 2: _____

_____

_____

_____

Action 3: _____

_____

_____

_____

Step 4: *Break down each action into a series of micro-actions:*

	Behavior	**When**	**Where**
1.	_____	_____	_____
	_____	_____	_____
	_____		
	_____		
	_____		
2.	_____	_____	_____
	_____	_____	_____
	_____		
	_____		
	_____		
3.	_____	_____	_____
	_____	_____	_____
	_____		
	_____		
	_____		

Step 5: *Track your progress over the next 8 weeks to see how well you*

Week 1	List of Weekly Actions	Mond	Tuesd	Wednesd	Thursd	Frida	Saturda	Sund

Week 2

List of Weekly Actions	Mond	Tuesd	Wednesd	Thursd	Frida	Saturda	Sund

Week 3

List of Weekly Actions	Mond	Tuesd	Wednesd	Thursd	Frida	Saturda	Sund

Week 4

List of Weekly Actions	Mond	Tuesd	Wednesd	Thursd	Frida	Saturda	Sund

List of Weekly Actions	Mond	Tuesd	Wednesd	Thursd	Frida	Saturda	Sund

Week 5

Week 6

List of Weekly Actions	Mond	Tuesd	Wednesd	Thursd	Frida	Saturda	Sund

Week 7

List of Weekly Actions	Mond	Tuesd	Wednesd	Thursd	Frida	Saturda	Sund

Week 8

List of Weekly Actions	Mond	Tuesd	Wednesd	Thursd	Frida	Saturda	Sund

Chapter 10

MOVING FORWARD AND EMBRACING YOUR SUCCESS

A s we have covered thus far, the path to liberate ourselves from feeling like an imposter when it comes to our own accomplishments is as follows:

Associated Chapter	Main Points Covered
1.	Identify the specific situations that trigger the feelings of imposter syndrome within us.
2.	Expand our self-awareness to understand the feelings/emotions that arise within us as a response to these triggers.
	Lessen our negative self-talk and empower ourselves to not be controlled by our internal chatter.
3.	Acknowledge, celebrate, and keep track of our small triumphs.
4.	Identify our unhealthy coping mechanism responses to challenges and setbacks and replace them with healthy ones.

Learn how to become more resilient to life's failures and disappointments.

5.   Use the power of affirmations to rewire our brain to make more positive connections, boost our confidence and give us some much-needed encouragement/motivation.

6.   Improve our self-reflection technique by leveraging the power of self-reflection journaling.

7.   Understand the importance of being able to ask our friends and family for support whenever we need it.

8.   Understand the critical role that low-self esteem and low self-confidence plays in preventing us from reaching our goals and perpetuating the negative feelings that accompany imposter syndrome.

        Identify our own strengths and weaknesses.

        Learn to describe ourselves in an objective/unbiased way.

9.   Learn how to use certain behavioral tools to help us start and finish the actions that are necessary to achieve our goals and make real changes in our lives.

Although these steps provide us with the keys to unlock the door to escape the perils of imposter syndrome, there is still one final piece of information that we must consider if we are to be truly liberated from being a perpetual imposter. The last puzzle piece is this: You must come to terms with both the good and bad in life and learn to accept the positive and negative traits within yourself. Negative feelings and negative situations are not something to escape from but are simply learning experiences that help us become more resilient, adaptable and achieve eventual success in our endeavors.

One of the biggest mistakes people make when it comes to fighting imposter syndrome is that they assume the main objective is to erase all negative thoughts and avoid all negative situations at all costs. This could not be further from the truth. Being overly positive (also referred to as 'toxic positivity') has just as many negative consequences as being overly negative. When it comes to ridding ourselves of imposter syndrome, the aim should be to restore the balance between our negative and positive thoughts, and then learn to maintain equilibrium between the two. Learning to accept the existence of the good and bad within ourselves builds our emotional intelligence and self-esteem. It accelerates our personal development, makes us more resilient to life's challenges and it is probably the most liberating thing that you can do for yourself as an 'imposter'.

In addition, remember that imposter syndrome is not actually a mental health condition. It is a set of learned patterns of behavior (mental and behavioral habits) that are a consequence of years of emotional conditioning. Unfortunately, this isn't necessarily good news. Anyone who has tried to break a bad habit before – for example, nail biting, smoking, swearing, or obsessive hair pulling (trichotillomania) – knows how difficult it is to not relapse back into our old habits. It's entirely possible to commit to freeing ourselves from the thoughts and feelings associated with imposter syndrome…. and succeed for a long time too! However, it is also entirely possible to relapse back into negative thinking after a short time (and sometimes the relapses can last for months at a time). This temporary display of weakness can make us feel shame, disappointment and guilt. We might even have second thoughts about whether we are truly capable of self-improvement.

The thing is, more than likely, most of us will relapse at least once. Luckily, relapsing gives us a rare opportunity for self-reflection. That is, we get to learn more about our thought processes and emotional tendencies when we transition from success to failure, and vice versa. This opportunity for deep self-learning also provides a valuable lesson in self-compassion and self-acceptance. We learn that it is perfectly normal to be inefficient one moment and efficient in the next, powerless in one situation and powerful in another, or focused in one area and disorganized in another. We learn to humble ourselves as we accept that it is impossible to avoid all setbacks and that is ok. We wouldn't want to live in a world where nighttime didn't exist. Or where it was only summer all year round. We need constant change and duality to truly enjoy the essence of life. After all, if it wasn't possible to fail, then would success even matter?

In fact, some would even argue that the most potent successes can only be achieved through failure. Learning to transition back to our good habits after a relapse is a technique that in many ways is quite similar to falling off a bicycle while learning to ride. For some, if they fall enough times, they simply give up. For others, if they fall enough times, it stops looking like 'falling' and starts to look like 'fancy bicycle tricks'. When we relapse, we don't need to exhaust ourselves by trying to fight it. On the contrary, we should allow ourselves to fully experience the fall back into our old ways, so that it isn't just an event that 'happens to us'. Instead, we assume more control over the descent back into our old ways each and every time it happens. Soon, we can expertly identify the triggers that can send us relapsing and avoid them with precision.

EXERCISE 10 – LEARNING HOW TO BOUNCE BACK WHEN WE RELAPSE INTO OUR OLD THINKING AND BEHAVIORAL PATTERNS

1. Let's start by assessing how far you've come in all of the areas that we have previously highlighted. On a scale of one to ten, with 1 being the least progress and 10 being the most progress, how much progress have you made in each area specified below?

Progress Area #1: I can identify the specific situations that trigger my feelings of being an imposter.

	1	2	3	4	5	6	7	8	9	10	
I have not made any progress in this area.	( )	( )	( )	( )	( )	( )	( )	( )	( )	( )	I have made significant progress in this area.

Progress Area #2: I can understand the feelings/emotions that arise in me as a response to these triggers.

	1	2	3	4	5	6	7	8	9	10	
I have not made any progress in this area.	( )	( )	( )	( )	( )	( )	( )	( )	( )	( )	I have made significant progress in this area.

Progress Area #3: I feel like I have more control over my internal chatter, and I can effectively lessen my negative self-talk.

	1	2	3	4	5	6	7	8	9	10	
I have not made any progress in this area.	( )	( )	( )	( )	( )	( )	( )	( )	( )	( )	I have made significant progress in this area.

Progress Area #4: I have taken the time to acknowledge, celebrate and keep track of my small wins.

	1	2	3	4	5	6	7	8	9	10	
I have not made any progress in this area.	( )	( )	( )	( )	( )	( )	( )	( )	( )	( )	I have made significant progress in this area.

Progress Area #5: I can identify my unhealthy coping mechanism responses to challenges and setbacks.

	1	2	3	4	5	6	7	8	9	10	
I have not made any progress in this area.	( )	( )	( )	( )	( )	( )	( )	( )	( )	( )	I have made significant progress in this area.

Progress Area #6: I can effectively replace my unhealthy coping mechanism responses with healthier ones.

	1	2	3	4	5	6	7	8	9	10	
I have not made any progress in this area.	( )	( )	( )	( )	( )	( )	( )	( )	( )	( )	I have made significant progress in this area.

Progress Area #7: I am more resilient to life's failures and disappointments.

	1	2	3	4	5	6	7	8	9	10	
I have not made any progress in this area.	( )	( )	( )	( )	( )	( )	( )	( )	( )	( )	I have made significant progress in this area.

Progress Area #8: I can effectively use positive affirmations to feel more empowered, boost my confidence and motivation.

1	2	3	4	5	6	7	8	9	10

I have not made any progress in this area.   ( ) ( ) ( ) ( ) ( ) ( ) ( ) ( ) ( ) ( )   I have made significant progress in this area.

Progress Area #9: I can effectively use journaling as a tool to improve my self-reflection technique.

1	2	3	4	5	6	7	8	9	10

I have not made any progress in this area.   ( ) ( ) ( ) ( ) ( ) ( ) ( ) ( ) ( ) ( )   I have made significant progress in this area.

Progress Area #10: I can effectively ask friends and family for

1	2	3	4	5	6	7	8	9	10

I have not made any progress in this area.   ( ) ( ) ( ) ( ) ( ) ( ) ( ) ( ) ( ) ( )   I have made significant progress in this area.

Progress Area #11: I can understand the role that my self-esteem and self confidence plays in helping me to reach my goals.

1	2	3	4	5	6	7	8	9	10

I have not made any progress in this area.   ( ) ( ) ( ) ( ) ( ) ( ) ( ) ( ) ( ) ( )   I have made significant progress in this area.

Progress Area #12: I can effectively identify my own strengths and weaknesses.

	1	2	3	4	5	6	7	8	9	10	
I have not made any progress in this area.	( )	( )	( )	( )	( )	( )	( )	( )	( )	( )	I have made significant progress in this area.

Progress Area #13: I can describe myself in an objective and unbiased way.

	1	2	3	4	5	6	7	8	9	10	
I have not made any progress in this area.	( )	( )	( )	( )	( )	( )	( )	( )	( )	( )	I have made significant progress in this area.

Progress Area #14: I can start and finish the actions that are necessary to achieve my goals.

	1	2	3	4	5	6	7	8	9	10	
I have not made any progress in this area.	( )	( )	( )	( )	( )	( )	( )	( )	( )	( )	I have made significant progress in this area.

2. In which area(s) are you currently relapsing?

Progress Area #: _____

_____

_____

3. *Can you identify the specific situation (s) that triggered your relapse into your old thinking and/or behavioral patterns?*

_____

_____

_____

4. *Describe the feelings and emotions that you are now experiencing because of this relapse.*

_____

_____

_____

5. *How are you coping with the feelings and emotions described above?*

_____

_____

_____

6. *Which of the following tools/techniques do you believe would be the most useful in helping you to bounce back from these negative emotions? (Feel free to select multiple options if you wish)*

( ) Chapter 2: Work on lessening my negative self-talk.

( ) Chapter 3: Focus on acknowledging and celebrating my recent small wins.

( ) Chapter 4: Replace my unhealthy coping mechanism responses with healthy ones.

( ) Chapter 5: Create affirmations to help empower and motivate me.

( ) Chapter 6: Start journaling and self-reflecting on what has happened.

( ) Chapter 7: Ask my friends and family for support.

( ) Chapter 8: Describe my strengths and weaknesses in an unbiased way.

( ) Chapter 9: Use micro-actions to get back on track with my goals.

7. *What are the potential consequences of not taking any of the actions listed above?*

_____

_____

_____

8. *What lessons have you learned about your transition from **success** (motivation, commitment, effort) to **failure** (mistakes, disappointment, inaction) and vice versa?*

_____

_____

_____

9. *What is the probability/likelihood that these events will occur again in the future?*

_____

_____

_____

10. *Are there any alternative actions that you could have taken to change the outcome of your current situation?*

_____

_____

_____

REFERENCES

Branden, N. (1995). *The Six Pillars of Self-Esteem: The Definitive Work on Self-Esteem by the Leading Pioneer in the Field.* Bantam; Reprint edition.

Branden, N. (2001). *The Psychology of Self-Esteem: A Revolutionary Approach to Self-Understanding that Launched a New Era in Modern Psychology.* Jossey-Bass; 1st edition.

Brown, B. (2010). *The Gifts of Imperfection: Let Go of Who You Think You're Supposed to Be and Embrace Who You Are.* Hazelden Publishing.

Carlson, R. (1997). *Don't Sweat the Small Stuff . . . and It's All Small Stuff: Simple Ways to Keep the Little Things from Taking Over Your Life.* Hachette Books; 1st edition.

Clance, D. P. (1985). *he Impostor Phenomenon: Overcoming the Fear That Haunts Your Success.* Peachtree Publishers.

Clear, J. (2018). *Atomic Habits: An Easy & Proven Way to Build Good Habits & Break Bad Ones.* Avery.

Covey, S. (2013). *The 7 Habits of Highly Effective People: Powerful Lessons in Personal Change.* Simon & Schuster; Anniversary edition.

Csikszentmihalyi, M. (2008). *Flow: The Psychology of Optimal Experience.* Harper Perennial Modern Classics; 1st edition.

Duhigg, C. (2014). *The Power of Habit: Why We Do What We Do in Life and Business.* Random House Trade Paperbacks.

Fennell, M. (1999). *Overcoming Low Self-Esteem : Self-Help Guide Using Cognitive Behavioural Techniques.* Robinson Publishing; 1st Edition.

Goleman, D. (2005). *Emotional Intelligence: Why It Can Matter More Than IQ.* Random House Publishing Group; 10th Anniversary edition.

Hawkes, S. (2017). *Chasing Perfection--: Shatter The Illusion; Minimize Self-Doubt & Maximize Success.* Advantage Media Group.

Hayes, S. (2005). *Get Out of Your Mind and Into Your Life: The New Acceptance and Commitment Therapy.* New Harbinger Publications; 1st edition.

Hibberd, J. (2019). *The Imposter Cure: Escape the Mind-Trap of Imposter Syndrome.* Aster.

Hollins, P. (2018). *Finish What You Start: The Art of Following Through, Taking Action, Executing, & Self-Discipline (Live a Disciplined Life).* CreateSpace Independent Publishing Platform.

Hunt, J. (2020). *Unlocking Your Authentic Self: Overcoming Impostor Syndrome, Enhancing Self-confidence, and Banishing Self-doubt.* JenniferHuntMD.

McKay, M. (2016). *Self-Esteem: A Proven Program of Cognitive Techniques for Assessing, Improving, and Maintaining Your Self-Esteem.* New Harbinger Publications; Fourth edition.

Meyer, J. (2002). *Battlefield of the Mind: Winning the Battle in Your Mind.* Warner Faith; Revised edition.

Orbé-Austin, L. (2020). *Own Your Greatness: Overcome Impostor Syndrome, Beat Self-Doubt, and Succeed in Life.* Ulysses Press.

Padesky, C., & Greenberger, D. (2015). *Mind Over Mood: Change How You Feel by Changing the Way You Think.* The Guilford Press; Second edition.

Peale, N. V. (2003). *The Power of Positive Thinking.* Touchstone; Reprint edition.

Spiegel, C. (2018). *A Year of Positive Thinking: Daily Inspiration, Wisdom, and Courage (A Year of Daily Reflections).* Althea Press.

Wiest, B. (2020). *The Mountain Is You: Transforming Self-Sabotage Into Self-Mastery.* Thought Catalog Books.

Young, V. (2011). *The Secret Thoughts of Successful Women: Why Capable People Suffer from the Impostor Syndrome and How to Thrive in Spite of It.* New York: Currency; Standard Edition.

Made in United States
Orlando, FL
13 September 2023